Growing in the Gospel

# The Psalms Project Volume Thirteen

*Discovering the Spiritual World through the Psalms – Psalm 121 - 150*

Michael Harvey Koplitz

# TABLE OF CONTENTS

## The goal of this project:

This research project will examine the 150 psalms for the spiritual awareness each Psalm offers. Each Psalm will be examined by its language and the commentary of the Sages. The spiritual awareness analysis will be done in alignment with Ari's definition of the Tree of life, the Book of Creation, and the Zohar. Each verse of the Psalm will be rewritten using the intent of the language and spiritual commentary to convey its spiritual lesson.

## The main resources:

The Zohar

The Book of Creation

Ari's writing on the Tree of Life and the Ten Sefirot

The Theological Wordbook of the Old Testament

Samson Hirsch's commentary on the Psalms

Tehillim – Psalms – A new translation with a commentary anthologized from the Talmudic and rabbinic sources

Accordance Bible Software

# Psalm 121

| New American Standard 1995 | Hebrew |
|---|---|

**Psa. 121:0**   A Song of Ascents.

**Psa. 121:1**   I will *[a]*lift up my eyes to *[b]*the mountains;
From where shall my help come?
2   My *[a]*help *comes* from the LORD,
Who *[b]*made heaven and earth.
3   He will not *[a]*allow your foot to slip;
He who *[b]*keeps you will not slumber.
4   Behold, He who keeps Israel
Will neither slumber nor sleep.

**Psa. 121:5**   The LORD is your *[a]*keeper;
The LORD is your *[b]*shade on your right hand.
6   The *[a]*sun will not smite you by day,
Nor the moon by night.
7   The LORD will *[1a]*protect you from all evil;
He will keep your soul.
8   The LORD will *[1a]*guard your going out and your coming in
*[b]*From this time forth and forever.

שִׁיר לַמַּעֲלוֹת אֶשָּׂא עֵינַי **Psa. 121:1**
אֶל־הֶהָרִים מֵאַיִן יָבֹא עֶזְרִי ׃ 2
עֶזְרִי מֵעִם יְהוָה עֹשֵׂה שָׁמַיִם
וָאָרֶץ ׃ 3 אַל־יִתֵּן לַמּוֹט רַגְלֶךָ אַל־
יָנוּם שֹׁמְרֶךָ ׃ 4 הִנֵּה לֹא־יָנוּם וְלֹא
יִישָׁן שׁוֹמֵר יִשְׂרָאֵל ׃ 5 יְהוָה שֹׁמְרֶךָ
יְהוָה צִלְּךָ עַל־יַד יְמִינֶךָ ׃ 6 יוֹמָם
הַשֶּׁמֶשׁ לֹא־יַכֶּכָּה וְיָרֵחַ בַּלָּיְלָה ׃ 7
יְהוָה יִשְׁמָרְךָ מִכָּל־רָע יִשְׁמֹר אֶת־
נַפְשֶׁךָ ׃ 8 יְהוָה יִשְׁמָר־צֵאתְךָ
וּבוֹאֶךָ מֵעַתָּה וְעַד־עוֹלָם ׃

# References

**Psalm 121:1**
[a]Ps 123:1; Is 40:26
[b]Ps 87:1

**Psalm 121:2**
[a]Ps 124:8
[b]Ps 115:15

**Psalm 121:3**
[a]1 Sam 2:9; Ps 66:9
[b]Ps 41:2; 127:1; Is 27:3

**Psalm 121:5**
[a]Ps 91:4
[b]Ps 16:8; 91:1; Is 25:4

**Psalm 121:6**
[a]Ps 91:5; Is 49:10; Jon 4:8; Rev 7:16

**Psalm 121:7**
[1]Or *keep*
[a]Ps 41:2; 91:10-12

**Psalm 121:8**
[1]Or *keep*
[a]Deut 28:6
[b]Ps 113:2; 115:18

## Targum

**Psa. 121:1** A song that was uttered on the ascents of the abyss. I will lift up my eyes to the mountains. Whence shall come my help? **2** My help is from the presence of the LORD, who made heaven and earth. **3** He will not allow your foot to falter, your guardian does not slumber. **4** Behold, he does not slumber and he will not sleep, the guardian of Israel. **5** The LORD will guard you, the LORD will overshadow you, on account of the mezuzah affixed on your right side as you enter. **6** By day, when the sun rules, the morning-demons will not smite you, nor will the liliths, at night, when the moon rules. **7** The word of the LORD will guard you from all harm, he will guard your soul. **8** The LORD will guard your going out for business and your coming in to study Torah, from now and forevermore.

## Spiritual Awareness

Introduction

This Psalm is not called a song of Ascents but is dedicated to the Ascents. Israel finds strength to attain divine heights and will ascend to the LORD's glorious presence. To do this, Israel must abandon its faith in earthly powers and lift its eyes to the LORD. Mortal protectors of the people are failing and unreliable.

Notes of the Psalm

The entire Psalm is a spiritual awareness song that every person who wishes to ascend into Heaven and be in the LORD's presence needs to understand. It is not the powers of the Earth, that are mortal powers, that will bring a person into Heaven. Rather, it will be one's trust and faith in the LORD that will offer salvation. The psalmist says it is up to the individual whether the person will arrive in Heaven when the time is over on Earth.

# Psalm 122

| New American Standard 1995 | Hebrew |
| --- | --- |

**Psa. 122:0**  A Song of Ascents, of David.

**Psa. 122:1**  I was glad when they said to me,
"Let us *go to the house of the LORD."
2  Our feet are standing
Within your *gates, O Jerusalem,
3  Jerusalem, that is *built
As a city that is *compact together;
4  To which the tribes *go up, even the tribes of [1]the LORD —
[2]An ordinance for Israel —
To give thanks to the name of the LORD.
5  For there *thrones were set for judgment,
The thrones of the house of David.

**Psa. 122:6**  Pray for the *peace of Jerusalem:
"May they prosper who *love you.
7  "May peace be within your *walls,
And prosperity within your *palaces."
8  For the sake of my *brothers and my friends,
I will now say, "*May peace be within you."
9  For the sake of the house of the LORD our God,
I will *seek your good.

שִׁיר הַמַּעֲלוֹת לְדָוִד **Psa. 122:1**
שָׂמַחְתִּי בְּאֹמְרִים לִי בֵּית יְהוָה
נֵלֵךְ ׃ 2 עֹמְדוֹת הָיוּ רַגְלֵינוּ
בִּשְׁעָרַיִךְ יְרוּשָׁלָ͏ִם ׃ 3 יְרוּשָׁלַ͏ִם
הַבְּנוּיָה כְּעִיר שֶׁחֻבְּרָה־לָּהּ יַחְדָּו ׃ 4
שֶׁשָּׁם עָלוּ שְׁבָטִים שִׁבְטֵי־יָהּ עֵדוּת
לְיִשְׂרָאֵל לְהֹדוֹת לְשֵׁם יְהוָה ׃ 5 כִּי
שָׁמָּה ׀ יָשְׁבוּ כִסְאוֹת לְמִשְׁפָּט
כִּסְאוֹת לְבֵית דָּוִיד ׃ 6 שַׁאֲלוּ שְׁלוֹם
יְרוּשָׁלָ͏ִם יִשְׁלָיוּ אֹהֲבָיִךְ ׃ 7 יְהִי־
שָׁלוֹם בְּחֵילֵךְ שַׁלְוָה בְּאַרְמְנוֹתָיִךְ ׃
8 לְמַעַן אַחַי וְרֵעָי אֲדַבְּרָה־נָּא
שָׁלוֹם בָּךְ ׃ 9 לְמַעַן בֵּית־יְהוָה
אֱלֹהֵינוּ אֲבַקְשָׁה טוֹב לָךְ ׃

# References

**Psalm 122:1**
*a*Ps 42:4; Is 2:3; Mic 4:2; Zech 8:21

**Psalm 122:2**
*a*Ps 9:14; 87:2; 116:19; Jer 7:2

**Psalm 122:3**
*a*Ps 48:13; 147:2
*b*2 Sam 5:9; Neh 4:6

**Psalm 122:4**
[1]Heb *YAH*
[2]Or *A testimony*
*a*Ex 23:17; Deut 16:16; Ps 84:5

**Psalm 122:5**
*a*Deut 17:8; 2 Chr 19:8; Ps 89:29

**Psalm 122:6**
*a*Ps 29:11; Jer 29:7
*b*Ps 102:14

**Psalm 122:7**
*a*Ps 51:18; Is 62:6
*b*Ps 48:3, 13; Jer 17:27

**Psalm 122:8**
*a*Ps 133:1
*b*1 Sam 25:6; John 20:19

**Psalm 122:9**
*a*Neh 2:10; Esth 10:3

## Targum

**Psa. 122:1** A song that was uttered on the ascents of the abyss. I rejoiced with those who say to me, "Let us go to the sanctuary of the LORD." **2** Our feet were standing in your gates, O Jerusalem. **3** Jerusalem that is built in the firmament is like a city that has been joined together on earth. **4** Unto which the tribes have gone up, the tribes of the LORD, he who testifies to Israel that his presence abides among them when they go to give thanks to the name of the LORD. **5** For there thrones have been placed; in Jerusalem thrones are in the sanctuary for the kings of the house of David. **6** Seek the welfare of Jerusalem; those who love you will dwell in tranquillity. **7** Let there be peace in your armies, tranquillity in your citadels. **8** On account of my brothers and companions, I will now speak in you of peace. **9** Because of the sanctuary of the LORD our God, I will seek to do good to you.

## Spiritual Awareness

### Introduction

This Psalm describes the glory of Jerusalem of old. In ancient days, cities generally remained small. Jerusalem on the other hand grew and grew. It was a place that a Jew could have a personal encounter with the LORD. That experience was a personal dramatic revelation which touched a different part of the soul. The different people who came to Jerusalem demonstrated the diversity of the LORD's creation. No one was concerned about skin color or nationality. If you came to Jerusalem to experience the LORD, especially when the Temples existed, the traveler was shown hospitality and immediate acceptance.

### Notes of the Psalm

In ancient days the people of Jerusalem truly followed the Torah. Hospitality was a mainstay of Semitic life. Nationality or race was not a concern to the people. The Children of Israel were descendants of Jacob and there were twelve tribes. All tribes of Israel were welcomed in Jerusalem. Also, people from all over the world who wanted to experience the love and grace of the LORD were welcomed. The Temple's outer court was especially designated for the non-Jew. These people had access to the LORD there. Many Jews came to the Temple and from the Gentile Court also felt the presence of the LORD. It was a time of acceptance of all people. Unfortunately, that is not what is happening today. The world would be much better off if the attitude of full acceptance and hospitality came back to the world.

# Psalm 123

| New American Standard 1995 | Hebrew |
|---|---|

**Psa. 123:0**   A Song of Ascents.

**Psa. 123:1**   To You I [a]lift up my eyes,
O You who [b]are enthroned in the heavens!
2   Behold, as the eyes of [a]servants *look* to the hand of their master,
As the eyes of a maid to the hand of her mistress,
So our [b]eyes *look* to the LORD our God,
Until He is gracious to us.

**Psa. 123:3**   [a]Be gracious to us, O LORD, be gracious to us,
For we are greatly filled [b]with contempt.
4   Our soul is greatly filled
With the [a]scoffing of [b]those who are at ease,
*And* with the [c]contempt of the proud.

שִׁיר הַֽמַּעֲלוֹת אֵלֶיךָ **Psa. 123:1**

נָשָׂאתִי אֶת־עֵינַי הַיֹּשְׁבִי בַּשָּׁמָיִם ׃ 2

הִנֵּה כְעֵינֵי עֲבָדִים אֶל־יַד

אֲדוֹנֵיהֶם כְּעֵינֵי שִׁפְחָה אֶל־יַד

גְּבִרְתָּהּ כֵּן עֵינֵינוּ אֶל־יְהוָה

אֱלֹהֵינוּ עַד שֶׁיְּחָנֵּנוּ ׃ 3 חָנֵּנוּ יְהוָה

חָנֵּנוּ כִּי־רַב שָׂבַעְנוּ בוּז ׃ 4 רַבַּת

שָׂבְעָה־לָּהּ נַפְשֵׁנוּ הַלַּעַג הַשַּׁאֲנַנִּים

הַבּוּז לִגְאֵיוֹנִים ׃

## References

**Psalm 123:1**
[a]Ps 121:1; 141:8
[b]Ps 2:4; 11:4

**Psalm 123:2**
[a]Prov 27:18; Mal 1:6
[b]Ps 25:15

**Psalm 123:3**
[a]Ps 4:1; 51:1
[b]Neh 4:4; Ps 119:22

**Psalm 123:4**
[a]Neh 2:19; Ps 79:4
[b]Job 12:5; Is 32:9, 11; Amos 6:1
[c]Neh 4:4; Ps 119:22

## Targum

**Psa. 123:1** A song that was uttered on the ascents of the abyss. Before you I have lifted up my eyes, you who sit on a throne of glory in heaven. [2] Behold, as the eyes of menservants, on one side, watch at the hands of their masters; and as the eyes of maidservants, on the other side, watch at the hands of their mistresses; thus our eyes watch in the presence of the LORD our God for the time when he will show compassion to us. [3] Have compassion on us, O LORD, have compassion on us; for we have had too much of contempt. [4] Our soul has had too much of scorn, for the arrogant and proud are at ease.

## Spiritual Awareness

Introduction

This Psalm discusses the reason that the LORD expelled Israel from the Promised Land. The people had displayed behaviors that are an abomination to the LORD. Therefore, the LORD was compelled to send Israel into Exile. While in Babylon, they purged these negative traits from their character. Arrogance (Proverbs 16:5), and haughty of heart (Proverbs 16:4) are traits that are abhorrent. The Psalmist also speaks about how humbled Israel in Exile came to acknowledge their full dependence upon the LORD.

Notes on the Psalm

There are plenty of human behaviors that are abhorrent to the LORD. The LORD's gift to us is the Bible. In these sacred writings is the list of behaviors that the LORD considers abhorrent. The Bible must be viewed as a gift. Yes, it has some Laws in it. However, the laws are there to help humanity in its quest to get closer to Heaven. Today there are people, including clergy, who want to disregard the Bible as an ancient book of stories. If this is allowed to happen then what guide does humanity have to please the LORD? The answer is obvious, none. The Bible must be held up as a sacred document which never changes. Learn how to please the LORD because it is necessary for the soul to return to Heaven.

The 4/5 soul (there are five parts to the soul according to the Zohar) comes to Malkhut (Earth) to join its 1/5 parts which is the flesh. As a complete soul, the objective is to learn about the LORD and to show the LORD that the soul wants to return to Heaven and serve Him. This can only occur by following the LORD's word (the sacred Bible). To follow human made institutions or artificial documents is the path to Sheol (Hell). Let no one tell you to toss out the Bible.

# Psalm 124

| New American Standard 1995 | Hebrew |
| --- | --- |

**Psa. 124:0**　A Song of Ascents, of David.

**Psa. 124:1**　"*a*Had it not been the LORD who was on our side,"
　　*b*Let Israel now say,
2　　"Had it not been the LORD who was on our side
　　When men rose up against us,
3　　Then they would have *a*swallowed us alive,
　　When their *b*anger was kindled against us;
4　　Then the *a*waters would have engulfed us,
　　The stream would have ¹swept over our soul;
5　　Then the *a*raging waters would have ¹swept over our soul."

**Psa. 124:6**　Blessed be the LORD,
　　Who has not given us ¹to be *a*torn by their teeth.
7　　Our soul has *a*escaped *b*as a bird out of the *c*snare of the trapper;
　　The snare is broken and we have escaped.
8　　Our *a*help is in the name of the LORD,
　　Who *b*made heaven and earth.

שִׁיר הַמַּעֲלוֹת לְדָוִד לוּלֵי **Psa. 124:1**
יְהוָה שֶׁהָיָה לָנוּ יֹאמַר־נָא יִשְׂרָאֵל׃
² לוּלֵי יְהוָה שֶׁהָיָה לָנוּ בְּקוּם עָלֵינוּ
אָדָם׃ ³ אֲזַי חַיִּים בְּלָעוּנוּ בַּחֲרוֹת
אַפָּם בָּנוּ׃ ⁴ אֲזַי הַמַּיִם שְׁטָפוּנוּ
נַחְלָה עָבַר עַל־נַפְשֵׁנוּ׃ ⁵ אֲזַי עָבַר
עַל־נַפְשֵׁנוּ הַמַּיִם הַזֵּידוֹנִים׃ ⁶
בָּרוּךְ יְהוָה שֶׁלֹּא נְתָנָנוּ טֶרֶף
לְשִׁנֵּיהֶם׃ ⁷ נַפְשֵׁנוּ כְּצִפּוֹר נִמְלְטָה
מִפַּח יוֹקְשִׁים הַפַּח נִשְׁבָּר וַאֲנַחְנוּ
נִמְלָטְנוּ׃ ⁸ עֶזְרֵנוּ בְּשֵׁם יְהוָה עֹשֵׂה
שָׁמַיִם וָאָרֶץ׃

# References

**Psalm 124:1**
[a]Ps 94:17
[b]Ps 129:1

**Psalm 124:3**
[a]Num 16:30; Ps 35:25; 56:1; 57:3; Prov 1:12
[b]Gen 39:19; Ps 138:7

**Psalm 124:4**
[1]Or *passed over*
[a]Job 22:11; Ps 18:16; 32:6; 69:2; 144:7

**Psalm 124:5**
[1]Or *passed over*
[a]Job 38:11

**Psalm 124:6**
[1]Lit *as a prey to*
[a]Ps 27:2; Prov 30:14

**Psalm 124:7**
[a]Ps 141:10; 2 Cor 11:33; Heb 11:34
[b]Prov 6:5
[c]Ps 91:3; Hos 9:8

**Psalm 124:8**
[a]Ps 121:2
[b]Gen 1:1; Ps 134:3

## Targum

**Psa. 124:1** A song that was uttered on the ascents of the abyss, composed by David. Had it not been for the LORD who was our help – let Israel say now – [2] Had it not been for the word of the LORD who was our help, when a son of man rose against us – [3] Then they would have swallowed us while alive, when their anger grew strong against us. [4] Then the waters would have washed us away, sickness would have passed over our soul. [5] Then the king would have passed over our soul, he who is likened to the malicious waters of the sea. [6] Blessed is the name of the LORD, who has not handed us over as dead meat to their teeth. [7] Our soul is like a bird saved from the traps of the fowlers; the trap broke, and we have been saved. [8] Our help is in the name of the word of the LORD, who made heaven and earth.

## Spiritual Awareness

### Introduction

The Psalmist offers thanksgiving to the LORD for all His assistance for the Children of Israel. Israel has survived throughout the centuries despite her enemy's attempts to destroy her. In every generation an enemy of the LORD's people arose who tried to crush the soul of the holy nation. In every case the LORD's people have had victory from the Sefirah Netzach. In this Psalm the nations are compared to deep water. This water can drown people or can become strong enough to sweep enemies away.

### Notes on the Psalm

Too many people today believe that everything good that has happened to them in life is by their control alone. Indeed, the LORD has given us freewill. Therefore, our individual choices help drive our lives. However, the LORD will give us small nudges from time to time to drive our souls to a specific situation. Certain events occur which we call coincidence are not that but intentional pressures from the LORD. The question becomes, will the person react positively or ignore the nudge? That is the freewill part of the equation.

The saying is "when God closes a door, He opens a window." It is up to the person to see the window open and to take advantage of it. Randomness in the world will cause unexpected events to occur. When bad things happen, will you place your faith that the LORD will offer a nudge to greener pastures? If you acknowledge this fact, then you will be better off in life.

Look for the nudges from the LORD. The Shekinah is always with us transferring the LORD's wishes to us. Learn to listen for the voice of the Shekinah calling out to you. In such a busy and noisy world people tend to forget to listen.

# Psalm 125

| New American Standard 1995 | Hebrew |
|---|---|
| **Psa. 125:0**  A Song of Ascents.<br><br>**Psa. 125:1**  Those who trust in the LORD<br> Are as Mount Zion, which *a*cannot be moved but *b*abides forever.<br>2  As the mountains surround Jerusalem,<br> So *a*the LORD surrounds His people<br> *b*From this time forth and forever.<br>3  For the *a*scepter of wickedness shall not rest upon the ¹land of the righteous,<br> So that the righteous *b*will not put forth their hands to do wrong.<br><br>**Psa. 125:4**  *a*Do good, O LORD, to those who are good<br> And to those who are *b*upright in their hearts.<br>5  But as for those who *a*turn aside to their *b*crooked ways,<br> The LORD will lead them away with the *c*doers of iniquity.<br> *d*Peace be upon Israel. | שִׁיר הַמַּעֲלוֹת הַבֹּטְחִים **Psa. 125:1**<br>בַּיהוָה כְּהַר־צִיּוֹן לֹא־יִמּוֹט לְעוֹלָם<br>יֵשֵׁב ‏: ² יְרוּשָׁלִַם הָרִים סָבִיב לָהּ<br>וַיהוָה סָבִיב לְעַמּוֹ מֵעַתָּה וְעַד־<br>עוֹלָם ‏: ³ כִּי לֹא יָנוּחַ שֵׁבֶט הָרֶשַׁע<br>עַל גּוֹרַל הַצַּדִּיקִים לְמַעַן לֹא־<br>יִשְׁלְחוּ הַצַּדִּיקִים בְּעַוְלָתָה יְדֵיהֶם ‏:<br>⁴ הֵיטִיבָה יְהוָה לַטּוֹבִים וְלִישָׁרִים<br>בְּלִבּוֹתָם ‏: ⁵ וְהַמַּטִּים עֲקַלְקַלּוֹתָם<br>יוֹלִיכֵם יְהוָה אֶת־פֹּעֲלֵי הָאָוֶן<br>שָׁלוֹם עַל־יִשְׂרָאֵל ‏: |

# References

**Psalm 125:1**
[a]Ps 46:5
[b]Ps 61:7; Eccl 1:4

**Psalm 125:2**
[a]Zech 2:5
[b]Ps 121:8

**Psalm 125:3**
[1]Lit *lot*
[a]Ps 89:22; Prov 22:8; Is 14:5
[b]1 Sam 24:10; Ps 55:20; Acts 12:1

**Psalm 125:4**
[a]Ps 119:68
[b]Ps 7:10; 11:2; 32:11; 36:10; 94:15

**Psalm 125:5**
[a]Job 23:11; Ps 40:4; 101:3
[b]Prov 2:15; Is 59:8
[c]Ps 92:7; 94:4
[d]Ps 128:6; Gal 6:16

## Targum

**Psa. 125:1** A song that was uttered on the ascents of the abyss. The righteous who trust in the word of the LORD are like Mount Zion; it will not totter, it is inhabited forever. [2] Mountains are round about Jerusalem, and the word of the LORD is round about his people from this time and forever. [3] For the scepter of wickedness will not rest on the lot of the righteous, so that the righteous will not stretch out their hand to deceit. [4] Be good, O LORD, to the good, and to those upright in their heart. [5] But those who go astray following their perversity – the LORD will make them go to Gehenna; their portion is with the workers of deceit. Peace be upon Israel!

## Spiritual Awareness

Introduction

The defense and security of the Jewish nation is a matter of primary concern. Too often in history, Israel has been vulnerable and helpless. The Psalmist emphasizes that the true fortifications of the country in internalized when the people have full faith in the LORD.

Notes on the Psalm

As other Psalmist wrote, the author of Psalm 125 reminds the people that without the LORD they are vulnerable. Indeed, people today are vulnerable when they do not have the protection of the LORD with them. It requires faith and effort to obtain the LORD's protection. Once a person has the LORD's protection, it is imperative to keep it. The simple requirement from the LORD is to follow His ways as defined in the Bible.

# Psalm 126

| New American Standard | Hebrew |
|---|---|

**Psa. 126:0**    A Song of Ascents.

**Psa. 126:1**    When the LORD [a]brought back [1]the captive ones of Zion,
We were [b]like those who dream.
2    Then our [a]mouth was filled with laughter
And our [b]tongue with joyful shouting;
Then they said among the nations,
"The LORD has [c]done great things for them."
3    The LORD has done great things for us;
We are [a]glad.

**Psa. 126:4**    Restore our captivity, O LORD,
As the [1a]streams in the [2]South.
5    Those who sow in [a]tears shall reap with [b]joyful shouting.
6    He who goes to and fro weeping, carrying *his* bag of seed,
Shall indeed come again with a shout of joy, bringing his sheaves *with him*.

שִׁיר הַמַּעֲלוֹת בְּשׁוּב יְהוָה **Psa. 126:1**
אֶת־שִׁיבַת צִיּוֹן הָיִינוּ כְּחֹלְמִים׃ 2
אָז יִמָּלֵא שְׂחוֹק פִּינוּ וּלְשׁוֹנֵנוּ רִנָּה
אָז יֹאמְרוּ בַגּוֹיִם הִגְדִּיל יְהוָה
לַעֲשׂוֹת עִם־אֵלֶּה׃ 3 הִגְדִּיל יְהוָה
לַעֲשׂוֹת עִמָּנוּ הָיִינוּ שְׂמֵחִים׃ 4
שׁוּבָה יְהוָה אֶת־שְׁבוּתֵנוּ [שְׁבִיתֵנוּ]
כַּאֲפִיקִים בַּנֶּגֶב׃ 5 הַזֹּרְעִים
בְּדִמְעָה בְּרִנָּה יִקְצֹרוּ׃ 6 הָלוֹךְ יֵלֵךְ
וּבָכֹה נֹשֵׂא מֶשֶׁךְ־הַזָּרַע בֹּא־יָבוֹא
בְרִנָּה נֹשֵׂא אֲלֻמֹּתָיו׃

# References

**Psalm 126:1**
[1]Or *those who returned to*
[a]Ps 85:1; Jer 29:14; Hos 6:11
[b]Acts 12:9

**Psalm 126:2**
[a]Job 8:21
[b]Ps 51:14; Is 35:6
[c]1 Sam 12:24; Ps 71:19; Luke 1:49

**Psalm 126:3**
[a]Is 25:9; Zeph 3:14

**Psalm 126:4**
[1]Lit *stream-beds*
[2]Heb *Negev*
[a]Is 35:6; 43:19

**Psalm 126:5**
[a]Ps 80:5; Jer 31:9, 16; Lam 1:2
[b]Is 35:10; 51:11; 61:7; Gal 6:9

## Targum

**Psa. 126:1** A song that was uttered on the ascents of the abyss. When the LORD makes the exiles of Zion return, we were like the sick who were healed. **2** Then will our mouths be full of laughter, and our tongue with praise; then will they say among the Gentiles, "The LORD has done great good to these." **3** The LORD has done great good to us; we are joyful. **4** O LORD, make our exiles return, like a land that is made habitable when fountains of water flow during drought. **5** Those who sow with tears will harvest with praise. **6** He will surely go with weeping; the ox that bears a load of seed will surely come with praise, when he bears his sheaves and grazes on the young growth from the furrow.

## Spiritual Awareness

Introduction

This is a Psalm of Ascents that describes the highest level of Ascents. The final redemption will appear to be a dream, because the wonders which will accompany it will exceed Israel's wildest expectations. David wrote the psalm as a prophecy of what was to occur long after his death.

Notes on the Psalm

Verse one asks the LORD when the people in Exile will return to Mount Zion. When the people returned to Jerusalem, they rebuilt the city and a second Temple to the LORD. Today, this Psalm could apply to any individual. It is easy for a person to become disconnected from the LORD. This can occur when a person's expectations of what the LORD will provide exceeds what can happen. The "dark night of the soul" is an expression used to indicate a separation from the LORD. This Psalm can say that the LORD brought Israel back from Exile in Babylon (the dark place) back to Jerusalem and His presence. The LORD awaits for all souls who have left him to return.

# Psalm 127

| New American Standard 1995 | Hebrew |
|---|---|
| | |

**Psa. 127:0**   A Song of Ascents, of Solomon.

**Psa. 127:1**   Unless the LORD *builds the house,

    They labor in vain who build it;
    Unless the LORD *guards the city,
    The watchman keeps awake in vain.

2    It is vain for you to rise up early,
    To ¹retire late,
    To *eat the bread of ²painful labors;
    For He gives to His *beloved *even *in his* sleep.

**Psa. 127:3**   Behold, *children are a ¹gift of the LORD,

    The *fruit of the womb is a reward.

4    Like arrows in the hand of a *warrior,
    So are the children of one's youth.

5    How *blessed is the man whose quiver is full of them;
    *They will not be ashamed
    When they *speak with their enemies *in the gate.

**Psa. 127:1** שִׁיר הַמַּעֲלוֹת לִשְׁלֹמֹה
אִם־יְהוָה ׀ לֹא־יִבְנֶה בַיִת שָׁוְא ׀
עָמְלוּ בוֹנָיו בּוֹ אִם־יְהוָה לֹא־
יִשְׁמָר־עִיר שָׁוְא ׀ שָׁקַד שׁוֹמֵר ²
שָׁוְא לָכֶם ׀ מַשְׁכִּימֵי קוּם מְאַחֲרֵי־
שֶׁבֶת אֹכְלֵי לֶחֶם הָעֲצָבִים כֵּן יִתֵּן
לִידִידוֹ שֵׁנָא ׃ ³ הִנֵּה נַחֲלַת יְהוָה
בָּנִים שָׂכָר פְּרִי הַבָּטֶן ׃ ⁴ כְּחִצִּים
בְּיַד־גִּבּוֹר כֵּן בְּנֵי הַנְּעוּרִים ׃ ⁵
אַשְׁרֵי הַגֶּבֶר אֲשֶׁר מִלֵּא אֶת־
אַשְׁפָּתוֹ מֵהֶם לֹא־יֵבֹשׁוּ כִּי־יְדַבְּרוּ
אֶת־אוֹיְבִים בַּשָּׁעַר ׃

# References

**Psalm 127:1**
[a]Ps 78:69
[b]Ps 121:4

**Psalm 127:2**
[1]Lit *delay sitting*
[2]Lit *toils*
[a]Gen 3:17, 19
[b]Ps 60:5
[c]Job 11:18, 19; Prov 3:24; Eccl 5:12

**Psalm 127:3**
[1]Or *heritage*
[a]Gen 33:5; 48:4; Josh 24:3, 4; Ps 113:9
[b]Deut 7:13; 28:4; Is 13:18

**Psalm 127:4**
[a]Ps 112:2; 120:4

**Psalm 127:5**
[a]Ps 128:2, 3
[b]Prov 27:11
[c]Is 29:21; Amos 5:12
[d]Gen 34:20

## Targum

**Psa. 127:1** A song that was uttered on the ascents of the abyss, composed by Solomon. If the word of the LORD will not build the city, its builders labor in vain; if the word of the LORD is not guarding the city of Jerusalem, its guard has stayed awake in vain. **2** In vain will you trouble yourselves to rise early in the morning to do robbery, who stay up late to do fornication, who eat the bread of the poor for which they labored honestly and truly; the LORD will give sleep to those who love him. [ANOTHER TARGUM: The wicked say to the righteous, "It is wrong for you that you rise early and pray in the morning and stay up late in the evening to study the Torah, eating the bread of sorrow." The righteous reply, "Truly, the LORD gives to those who love him a complete reward for hunger."] **3** Behold, the legacy of the LORD is proper sons, children of the womb are a reward for good deeds. **4** Like arrows in the hand of a warrior, so are sons of the youth. **5** It is good for a man that he fill his academy with them; they will not be ashamed, for they will dispute with their enemies in the gate of the place of judgment.

## Spiritual Awareness

### Introduction

Divine assistance is essential for a person to succeed in any endeavor. How valuable is a person's work? Work brings out the genuine glory for those who toil in it (Nedarim 49b of the Talmud). Marriage and parenthood are the noblest pursuits of a person's life but only when the LORD is a part of it. The people in Exile were reminded of marriage, parenthood and labor because it gave them a purpose.

### Notes on the Psalm

It is a spiritual gift to have children if the parents will teach their children about the LORD. Without children, humanity dies out. If this happens, then everything that the LORD created was for nothing. The LORD created the Heavens and Earth so that He could create humanity and have a loving relationship with this Creation. Therefore, continuing the species is very important. Also, when teaching the ways of the LORD to one's children, the parent moves closer in their walk with the LORD. The Bible serves numerous purposes. Its Laws are there to teach us how to live a life that pleases the LORD. The Mitzvot when performed, stores spiritual gifts in Heaven for the soul. Teaching the Torah, prophets and writings to the children insures future generations will know about the love of the LORD.

# Psalm 128

| New American Standard 1995 | Hebrew |
|---|---|
| **Psa. 128:0**  A Song of Ascents.<br><br>**Psa. 128:1**  *a*How blessed is everyone who fears the LORD,<br>    Who *b*walks in His ways.<br>2    When you shall *a*eat of the *1b*fruit of your hands,<br>    You will be happy and *c*it will be well with you.<br>3    Your wife shall be like a *a*fruitful vine<br>    *1*Within your house,<br>    Your children like *b*olive plants<br>    Around your table.<br>4    Behold, for thus shall the man be blessed<br>    Who fears the LORD.<br><br>**Psa. 128:5**  *a*The LORD bless you *b*from Zion,<br>    And may you see the prosperity of Jerusalem all the days of your life.<br>6    Indeed, may you see your *a*children's children.<br>    *b*Peace be upon Israel! | שִׁיר הַמַּעֲלוֹת אַשְׁרֵי כָּל־ **Psa. 128:1**<br>יְרֵא יְהוָה הַהֹלֵךְ בִּדְרָכָיו ׃ ² יְגִיעַ<br>כַּפֶּיךָ כִּי תֹאכֵל אַשְׁרֶיךָ וְטוֹב לָךְ ׃<br>³ אֶשְׁתְּךָ ׀ כְּגֶפֶן פֹּרִיָּה בְּיַרְכְּתֵי<br>בֵיתֶךָ בָּנֶיךָ כִּשְׁתִלֵי זֵיתִים סָבִיב<br>לְשֻׁלְחָנֶךָ ׃ ⁴ הִנֵּה כִי־כֵן יְבֹרַךְ גָּבֶר<br>יְרֵא יְהוָה ׃ ⁵ יְבָרֶכְךָ יְהוָה מִצִּיּוֹן<br>וּרְאֵה בְּטוּב יְרוּשָׁלָ͏ִם כֹּל יְמֵי<br>חַיֶּיךָ ׃ ⁶ וּרְאֵה־בָנִים לְבָנֶיךָ שָׁלוֹם<br>עַל־יִשְׂרָאֵל ׃ |

## References

**Psalm 128:1**
[a]Ps 112:1; 119:1
[b]Ps 119:3

**Psalm 128:2**
[1]Lit *labor*
[a]Is 3:10
[b]Ps 109:11; Hag 2:17
[c]Eccl 8:12; Eph 6:3

**Psalm 128:3**
[1]Lit *In the innermost parts of*
[a]Ezek 19:10
[b]Ps 52:8; 144:12

**Psalm 128:5**
[a]Ps 134:3
[b]Ps 20:2; 135:21

**Psalm 128:6**
[a]Gen 48:11; 50:23; Job 42:16; Ps 103:17; Prov 17:6
[b]Ps 125:5

## Targum

**Psa. 128:1** A song that was uttered on the ascents of the abyss. How happy all who fear the LORD, who walk in his ways. ² [Happy] the work of your hands, for you will eat [it]; happy are you in this age and you shall have good in the age to come. ³ Your wife is like a vine that bore fruit on the side of your house; your sons are like olive plants around your table. ⁴ Behold, because of this, blessed is the man who is reverent in the presence of the LORD. ⁵ The LORD will bless you from Zion, and you will see the welfare of Jerusalem all the days of your life. ⁶ And you will see the sons of your sons. Peace be upon Israel.

## Spiritual Awareness

Introduction

This Psalm is a continuation of the previous one. Therefore, the introduction and notes about a spiritual awareness of Psalm 127 applies to Psalm 128.

# Psalm 129

| New American Standard 1995 | Hebrew |
|---|---|
| **Psa. 129:0**  A Song of Ascents.<br><br>**Psa. 129:1**  "[1]Many times they have [2a]persecuted me from my [b]youth up,"<br>    [c]Let Israel now say,<br>2    "[1]Many times they have [2]persecuted me from my youth up;<br>    Yet they have [a]not prevailed against me.<br>3    "The plowers plowed upon my back;<br>    They lengthened their furrows."<br>4    The LORD [a]is righteous;<br>    He has cut in two the [b]cords of the wicked.<br><br>**Psa. 129:5**  May all who [a]hate Zion<br>    Be [b]put to shame and turned backward;<br>6    Let them be like [a]grass upon the housetops,<br>    Which withers before it [1]grows up;<br>7    With which the reaper does not fill his [1]hand,<br>    Or the binder of sheaves his [a]bosom;<br>8    Nor do those who pass by say,<br>    "The [a]blessing of the LORD be upon you;<br>    We bless you in the name of the LORD." | שִׁיר הַֽמַּעֲלוֹת רַבַּת צְרָרוּנִי **Psa. 129:1**<br>מִנְּעוּרַי יֹאמַר־נָא יִשְׂרָאֵל׃ 2 רַבַּת<br>צְרָרוּנִי מִנְּעוּרָי גַּם לֹא־יָכְלוּ לִי׃ 3<br>עַל־גַּבִּי חָרְשׁוּ חֹרְשִׁים הֶאֱרִיכוּ<br>לְמַעֲנוֹתָם [ל][מַעֲנִיתָם ׃] 4 יְהוָה<br>צַדִּיק קִצֵּץ עֲבוֹת רְשָׁעִים׃ 5 יֵבֹשׁוּ<br>וְיִסֹּגוּ אָחוֹר כֹּל שֹׂנְאֵי צִיּוֹן׃ 6 יִהְיוּ<br>כַּחֲצִיר גַּגּוֹת שֶׁקַּדְמַת שָׁלַף יָבֵשׁ׃ 7<br>שֶׁלֹּא מִלֵּא כַפּוֹ קוֹצֵר וְחִצְנוֹ<br>מְעַמֵּר׃ 8 וְלֹא אָמְרוּ ׀ הָעֹבְרִים<br>בִּרְכַּת־יְהוָה אֲלֵיכֶם בֵּרַכְנוּ אֶתְכֶם<br>בְּשֵׁם יְהוָה׃ |

# References

**Psalm 129:1**
[1]Lit *Much*
[2]Lit *showed hostility toward*
[a]Ex 1:11; Judg 3:8; Ps 88:15
[b]Is 47:12; Jer 2:2; 22:21; Ezek 16:22; Hos 2:15; 11:1
[c]Ps 124:1

**Psalm 129:2**
[1]Lit *Much*
[2]Lit *showed hostility toward*
[a]Jer 1:19; 15:20; 20:11; Matt 16:18; 2 Cor 4:8, 9

**Psalm 129:4**
[a]Ps 119:137
[b]Ps 140:5

**Psalm 129:5**
[a]Mic 4:11
[b]Ps 70:3; 71:13

**Psalm 129:6**
[1]Lit *draws out*
[a]2 Kin 19:26; Ps 37:2; Is 37:27

**Psalm 129:7**
[1]Lit *palm*
[a]Ps 79:12

**Psalm 129:8**
[a]Ruth 2:4; Ps 118:26

## Targum

**Psa. 129:1** A song that was uttered on the ascents of the abyss. Many are they who have oppressed me from my youth – let Israel now say – **2** Many are they who have oppressed me from my youth, yet they have not been able to do me harm. **3** Upon my body the plowers have plowed, they have made their furrow long. **4** The LORD is righteous; he has severed the bonds of the wicked. **5** They will be ashamed and withdraw: all those who hate Zion. **6** They will be like the grass of the rooftops, which, before it blossoms, the east wind comes blowing on it and it has withered. **7** Which the reaper does not fill his hand with, nor the sheaver his shoulder. **8** And those who pass by do not say there, "The blessing of the LORD be upon you," nor will they answer, "We bless you in the name of the LORD."

## Spiritual Awareness

Introduction

The Psalmist encourages the reader to learn the annals of Jewish history. The diverse periods of history must not be viewed as separate occurrences but as one long lifetime. Every event in Israel's history is connected to some other event. It is also important to remember the painful times as well as the good times.

Notes on the Psalm

History repeats itself. The mistakes of the past are made over and over. The mistakes of the past need to be remembered so that they do not happen again. Covenants with the LORD are celebrated annually to remind the people of promises made. For example, the Passover and Shavuot are celebrated every year. This is to remind the people of the past events and the covenant that the LORD made with Israel. People like the circular year of events. It offers stability in an unstable world. People know when Nissan 1 comes that in fourteen days the Passover is celebrated. This gives people a side purpose of preparing for the celebration. The Passover celebration is a joyous time of the year because it commemorates Israel's freedom from the slavery of Egypt. Shavuot reminds the people of the day Moses received the Ten Commandments from the LORD. It is those events which bind the people to each other and to the LORD.

# Psalm 130

| New American Standard 1995 | Hebrew |
| --- | --- |

**Psa. 130:0**   A Song of Ascents.

**Psa. 130:1**        Out of the *a*depths I have cried to You, O LORD.

2        Lord, *a*hear my voice!
         Let *b*Your ears be attentive
         To the *c*voice of my supplications.

3        If You, [1]LORD, should mark iniquities,
         O Lord, who could *a*stand?

4        But there is *a*forgiveness with You,
         That You may be *b*feared.

**Psa. 130:5**        I wait for the LORD, my *a*soul does wait,
         And [1]*b*in His word do I hope.

6        My soul *waits* for the Lord
         More than the watchmen *a*for the morning;
         *Indeed, more than* the watchmen for the morning.

7        O Israel, *a*hope in the LORD;
         For with the LORD there is *b*lovingkindness,
         And with Him is *c*abundant redemption.

8        And He will *a*redeem Israel
         From all his iniquities.

שִׁיר הַמַּעֲלוֹת מִמַּעֲמַקִּים **Psa. 130:1**
קְרָאתִיךָ יְהוָה ׃ ² אֲדֹנָי שִׁמְעָה
בְקוֹלִי תִּהְיֶינָה אָזְנֶיךָ קַשֻּׁבוֹת
לְקוֹל תַּחֲנוּנָי ׃ ³ אִם־עֲוֹנוֹת תִּשְׁמָר־
יָהּ אֲדֹנָי מִי יַעֲמֹד ׃ ⁴ כִּי־עִמְּךָ
הַסְּלִיחָה לְמַעַן תִּוָּרֵא ׃ ⁵ קִוִּיתִי
יְהוָה קִוְּתָה נַפְשִׁי וְלִדְבָרוֹ
הוֹחָלְתִּי ׃ ⁶ נַפְשִׁי לַאדֹנָי מִשֹּׁמְרִים
לַבֹּקֶר שֹׁמְרִים לַבֹּקֶר ׃ ⁷ יַחֵל
יִשְׂרָאֵל אֶל־יְהוָה כִּי־עִם־יְהוָה
הַחֶסֶד וְהַרְבֵּה עִמּוֹ פְדוּת ׃ ⁸ וְהוּא
יִפְדֶּה אֶת־יִשְׂרָאֵל מִכֹּל עֲוֹנֹתָיו ׃

# References

**Psalm 130:1**
[a]Ps 42:7; 69:2; Lam 3:55

**Psalm 130:2**
[a]Ps 64:1; 119:149
[b]2 Chr 6:40; Neh 1:6, 11
[c]Ps 28:2; 140:6

**Psalm 130:3**
[1]Heb *YAH*
[a]Ps 76:7; 143:2; Nah 1:6; Mal 3:2; Rev 6:17

**Psalm 130:4**
[a]Ex 34:7; Neh 9:17; Ps 86:5; Is 55:7; Dan 9:9
[b]1 Kin 8:39, 40; Jer 33:8, 9

**Psalm 130:5**
[1]Lit *for*
[a]Ps 27:14; 33:20; 40:1; 62:1, 5; Is 8:17; 26:8
[b]Ps 119:74, 81

**Psalm 130:6**
[a]Ps 63:6; 119:147

**Psalm 130:7**
[a]Ps 131:3
[b]Ps 86:5; 103:4
[c]Ps 111:9; Rom 3:24; Eph 1:7

**Psalm 130:8**
[a]Ps 103:3, 4; Luke 1:68; Titus 2:14

## Targum

**Psa. 130:1** A song that was uttered on the ascents of the abyss. From the depths I have called you, O LORD. **2** O LORD, receive my prayer; may your ears be attentive to the sound of my prayer. **3** If you will take note of iniquities, O Yah, LORD, who will remain? **4** For there is forgiveness with you, so that you might be seen. **5** I have waited, O LORD; my soul has waited, and for his glory I have waited long. **6** My soul has waited long for the LORD, more than the watchmen on the morning watch who watch to offer the morning sacrifice. **7** Israel waits long for the LORD, for with the LORD is kindness, and with him is much redemption. **8** And he will redeem Israel from all his iniquities.

## Spiritual Awareness

Introduction

The Songs of Ascent raised human spirits. The message of hope was never more important than during the Exile. The worst part of the Exile was when the people accepted the fact that their behavior caused the LORD to remove His protection from them and thus the Babylonian came to Judea to conquer it. This military move destroyed the sacred city of Jerusalem and the First Temple to the LORD.

Verse four

The English versions of this psalm like to say "You may be feared." A proper translation is show reverence. The Psalmist says that one should indicate reverence to the LORD because only the LORD can forgive sins.

**For with You there is forgiveness so that You may be revered.**

Notes on the Psalm

Demonstrating reverence to the LORD is to obey the commandments and perform the mitzvot found in the Torah. It is actually a very simple formula. The Ten Commandments were written as a treaty. The LORD is the stronger partner. He said if Israel followed the Torah, then He would offer His protection. There a came a point in time that the LORD could no longer accept the sin of the people. Therefore, he sent the Babylonians to destruct the Temple because it was no longer sanctified to the LORD. Too much pagan worship was occurring in the Temple. The LORD sent the Babylonians to destroy the Temple that was once dedicated to Him.

# Psalm 131

| New American Standard 1995 | Hebrew |
|---|---|
| **Psa. 131:0**  A Song of Ascents, of David.<br><br>**Psa. 131:1**  O LORD, my heart is not [a]proud, nor my eyes [1][b]haughty;<br>Nor do I [2]involve myself in [c]great matters,<br>Or in things [d]too [3]difficult for me.<br>[2]  Surely I have [a]composed and quieted my soul;<br>Like a weaned [b]child *rests* [1]against his mother,<br>My soul is like a weaned child [1]within me.<br>[3]  O Israel, [a]hope in the LORD<br>[b]From this time forth and forever. | שִׁיר הַמַּעֲלוֹת לְדָוִד **Psa. 131:1** יְהוָה<br>לֹא־גָבַהּ לִבִּי וְלֹא־רָמוּ עֵינַי<br>וְלֹא־הִלַּכְתִּי בִּגְדֹלוֹת וּבְנִפְלָאוֹת<br>מִמֶּנִּי ‏2‏ אִם־לֹא שִׁוִּיתִי וְדוֹמַמְתִּי<br>נַפְשִׁי כְּגָמֻל עֲלֵי אִמּוֹ כַּגָּמֻל עָלַי<br>נַפְשִׁי ‏3‏ יַחֵל יִשְׂרָאֵל אֶל־יְהוָה<br>מֵעַתָּה וְעַד־עוֹלָם ׃ |

# References

**Psalm 131:1**
[1]Or *lofty*
[2]Lit *go after,* walk
[3]Or *marvelous*
[a]2 Sam 22:28; Ps 101:5; Is 2:12; Zeph 3:11
[b]Prov 30:13; Is 5:15
[c]Jer 45:5; Rom 12:16
[d]Job 42:3; Ps 139:6

**Psalm 131:2**
[1]Or *upon*
[a]Ps 62:1
[b]Matt 18:3; 1 Cor 14:20

**Psalm 131:3**
[a]Ps 130:7
[b]Ps 113:2

# Targum

**Psa. 131:1** A song uttered on the ascents of the abyss. O LORD, my heart is not proud, and my eyes are not lifted up, and I have not walked in things too great and wonderful for me. [2] Verily I have placed a hand on my mouth and silenced my soul while listening to words of Torah, like a weaned child at its mother's breasts; I have become mighty in the Torah; like a weaned child is my soul upon him. [3] Let Israel wait long for the LORD from now and forevermore.

## Spiritual Awareness

Introduction

In this Psalm, King David explores the depths of his own personality and reveals the innocent quality of his trusting soul. Even though David was a King, he approached the LORD with genuine humility and self-effacement. David foresaw that the Jews were destined to languish in Exile. David understood that the way to redemption from exile was to demonstrate humility before the LORD.

Notes of the Psalm

It does not matter what your position is in society, synagogue, or church. There is no rank in Heaven. Leaders must remember this as David did. David treated his people well. Too many world leaders do not treat their citizens well nor equal. Equality is supposed to exist. The same idea exists in houses of worship. Yes, there is leadership. The leaders have to remember that every member is equal!

# Psalm 132

| New American Standard 1995 | Hebrew |
| --- | --- |

**Psa. 132:0**   A Song of Ascents.

**Psa. 132:1**   Remember, O LORD, on David's behalf,
All [a]his affliction;
2   How he swore to the LORD
And vowed to [a]the Mighty One of Jacob,
3   "Surely I will not [1]enter [a]my house,
Nor [2]lie on my bed;
4   I will not [a]give sleep to my eyes
Or slumber to my eyelids,
5   Until I find a [a]place for the LORD,
[1]A dwelling place for [b]the Mighty One of Jacob."

**Psa. 132:6**   Behold, we heard of it in [a]Ephrathah,
We found it in the [b]field of [1]Jaar.
7   Let us go into His [1a]dwelling place;
Let us [b]worship at His [c]footstool.
8   [a]Arise, O LORD, to Your [b]resting place,
You and the ark of Your [c]strength.
9   Let Your priests be [a]clothed with righteousness,
And let Your [b]godly ones sing for joy.

**Psa. 132:10**   For the sake of David Your servant,
Do not turn away the face of Your [a]anointed.
11   The LORD has [a]sworn to David

שִׁיר הַמַּעֲלוֹת זְכוֹר־יְהוָה **Psa. 132:1**
לְדָוִד אֵת כָּל־עֻנּוֹתוֹ ׃ ² אֲשֶׁר
נִשְׁבַּע לַיהוָה נָדַר לַאֲבִיר יַעֲקֹב ׃ ³
אִם־אָבֹא בְּאֹהֶל בֵּיתִי אִם־אֶעֱלֶה
עַל־עֶרֶשׂ יְצוּעָי ׃ ⁴ אִם־אֶתֵּן שְׁנַת
לְעֵינָי לְעַפְעַפַּי תְּנוּמָה ׃ ⁵ עַד־
אֶמְצָא מָקוֹם לַיהוָה מִשְׁכָּנוֹת
לַאֲבִיר יַעֲקֹב ׃ ⁶ הִנֵּה־שְׁמַעֲנוּהָ
בְאֶפְרָתָה מְצָאנוּהָ בִּשְׂדֵי־יָעַר ׃ ⁷
נָבוֹאָה לְמִשְׁכְּנוֹתָיו נִשְׁתַּחֲוֶה לַהֲדֹם
רַגְלָיו ׃ ⁸ קוּמָה יְהוָה לִמְנוּחָתֶךָ
אַתָּה וַאֲרוֹן עֻזֶּךָ ׃ ⁹ כֹּהֲנֶיךָ יִלְבְּשׁוּ־
צֶדֶק וַחֲסִידֶיךָ יְרַנֵּנוּ ׃ ¹⁰ בַּעֲבוּר
דָּוִד עַבְדֶּךָ אַל־תָּשֵׁב פְּנֵי מְשִׁיחֶךָ ׃
¹¹ נִשְׁבַּע־יְהוָה לְדָוִד אֱמֶת לֹא־
יָשׁוּב מִמֶּנָּה מִפְּרִי בִטְנְךָ אָשִׁית
לְכִסֵּא־לָךְ ׃ ¹² אִם־יִשְׁמְרוּ בָנֶיךָ
בְּרִיתִי וְעֵדֹתִי זוֹ אֲלַמְּדֵם גַּם־
בְּנֵיהֶם עֲדֵי־עַד יֵשְׁבוּ לְכִסֵּא־לָךְ ׃
¹³ כִּי־בָחַר יְהוָה בְּצִיּוֹן אִוָּהּ לְמוֹשָׁב
לוֹ ׃ ¹⁴ זֹאת־מְנוּחָתִי עֲדֵי־עַד פֹּה־
אֵשֵׁב כִּי אִוִּתִיהָ ׃ ¹⁵ צֵידָהּ בָּרֵךְ
אֲבָרֵךְ אֶבְיוֹנֶיהָ אַשְׂבִּיעַ לָחֶם ׃ ¹⁶
וְכֹהֲנֶיהָ אַלְבִּישׁ יֶשַׁע וַחֲסִידֶיהָ רַנֵּן

A truth from which He will not turn back:

"[b]Of the fruit of your body I will set upon your throne.

12 "If your sons will keep My covenant

And My testimony which I will teach them,

Their sons also shall [a]sit upon your throne forever."

**Psa. 132:13** For the LORD has [a]chosen Zion;

He has [b]desired it for His habitation.

14 "This is My [a]resting place forever;

Here I will [b]dwell, for I have desired it.

15 "I will abundantly [a]bless her provision;

I will [b]satisfy her needy with bread.

16 "Her [a]priests also I will clothe with salvation,

And her [a]godly ones will sing aloud for joy.

17 "There I will cause the [a]horn of David to spring forth;

I have prepared a [b]lamp for Mine anointed.

18 "His enemies I will [a]clothe with shame,

But upon himself his [b]crown shall shine."

יְרַנֵּנוּ ׃ 17 שָׁם אַצְמִיחַ קֶרֶן לְדָוִד עָרַכְתִּי נֵר לִמְשִׁיחִי ׃ 18 אוֹיְבָיו אַלְבִּישׁ בֹּשֶׁת וְעָלָיו יָצִיץ נִזְרוֹ ׃

## References

**Psalm 132:1**
[a]Gen 49:24; 2 Sam 16:12

**Psalm 132:2**
[a]Gen 49:24; Is 49:26; 60:16

**Psalm 132:3**
[1]Lit *come into the tabernacle of*
[2]Lit *go up into the couch of*
[a]Job 21:28

**Psalm 132:4**
[a]Prov 6:4

**Psalm 132:5**
[1]Lit *Dwelling places*
[a]1 Kin 8:17; 1 Chr 22:7; Ps 26:8; Acts 7:46
[b]Ps 132:2

**Psalm 132:6**
[1]Or *the wood*
[a]Gen 35:19; 1 Sam 17:12
[b]1 Sam 7:1

**Psalm 132:7**
[1]Lit *dwelling places*
[a]Ps 43:3
[b]Ps 5:7; 99:5
[c]1 Chr 28:2

**Psalm 132:8**
[a]Num 10:35; 2 Chr 6:41; Ps 68:1
[b]Ps 132:14
[c]Ps 78:61

**Psalm 132:9**
[a]Job 29:14
[b]Ps 30:4; 132:16; 149:5

**Psalm 132:10**
[a]Ps 2:2; 132:17

**Psalm 132:11**
[a]Ps 89:3, 35
[b]2 Sam 7:12-16; 1 Chr 17:11-14; 2 Chr 6:16; Ps 89:4; Acts 2:30

**Psalm 132:12**
[a]Luke 1:32; Acts 2:30

**Psalm 132:13**
[a]Ps 48:1, 2; 78:68
[b]Ps 68:16

**Psalm 132:14**
[a]Ps 132:8
[b]Ps 68:16; Matt 23:21

**Psalm 132:15**
[a]Ps 147:14
[b]Ps 107:9

**Psalm 132:16**
[a]2 Chr 6:41; Ps 132:9

**Psalm 132:17**
[a]Ezek 29:21; Luke 1:69
[b]1 Kin 11:36; 15:4; 2 Kin 8:19; 2 Chr 21:7; Ps 18:28

**Psalm 132:18**
[a]Job 8:22; Ps 35:26; 109:29
[b]Ps 21:3

## Targum

**Psa. 132:1** A song that was uttered on the ascents of the abyss. Remember, O LORD, for David, all his affliction. <sup>2</sup> Who affirmed before the LORD a vow to the mighty one of Jacob. <sup>3</sup> I will not approach my wife, I will not ascend to the couch of my repose, <sup>4</sup> I will not give sleep to my eyes, slumber to my eyelids, <sup>5</sup> Until I find a place to build the sanctuary of the LORD, tents for the mighty one of Jacob. <sup>6</sup> Behold, we have heard it in Ephrat, we have found it in the field of the forests of Lebanon, the place where the fathers of old prayed. <sup>7</sup> Let us enter his tents, let us bow down to his footstool. <sup>8</sup> Arise, O LORD, abide in the dwelling-place of your rest, you and the ark in which is your Torah. <sup>9</sup> Your priests will wear clothing of righteousness, and your pious Levites will sing praise over your sacrifices. <sup>10</sup> Because of the merit of David your servant; when the ark comes through the middle of the gates, do not turn back the face of Solomon your anointed. <sup>11</sup> The LORD has affirmed to David in truth, he will not turn from it: "One of the children of your belly I will set as a king on your throne." <sup>12</sup> If your sons keep my covenant and this testimony of mine that I shall teach them, then your sons will forever sit on your throne. <sup>13</sup> For the LORD is pleased with Zion; he has desired it for his habitation. <sup>14</sup> This is the resting place of my presence forever; here I will dwell, for I have desired it. <sup>15</sup> Her provisions I will surely bless; and her needy shall have their fill of bread. <sup>16</sup> And her priests I will clothe in garments of redemption, and her pious will surely sing praise. <sup>17</sup> There I will cause to come forth a glorious king of the house of David; I have prepared a lamp for my anointed. <sup>18</sup> His enemies I will clothe with garments of shame; and his crown will glitter upon him.

## Spiritual Awareness

Introduction

King David longed to build the Temple to the LORD, the Beis HaMikdash. Although the LORD did not permit David to build the Temple he was granted the privilege of gathering the construction materials. David composed this Psalm in reference to three separate events which were all related to the Temple. In his youth David struggled to identify the precise spot where the altar of the Temple was to stand. Towards the end of his reign, David built an altar on that spot. Finally, it a Solomon who constructed the Temple so that David's altar to the LORD was its focal point.

Notes on this Psalm

For David the construction of the Temple to the LORD was paramount. David had been raised from a shepherd boy to become Israel's greatest King. David wanted to honor and worship the LORD above everything. The Temple became a sacred place where the children of Jacob could offer themselves to the LORD and know of His presence. Today there is not one centralized Temple but rather many smaller places of worship where the presence of the LORD can be sensed. If you attend worship at one of these places how much do you honor that house of the LORD. For David honoring the LORD was paramount. David knew that everything that he was and had came from the LORD. The average person today does not think that way. The presence of the LORD through the Shekinah can be felt anywhere. The strongest place to feel the Shekinah is in a place of worship that is dedicated to the LORD. However, the congregation in said place of worship must want this to happen. To many places of worship are country clubs. If you belong to such a place do what you can to change the attitude of the congregation to see their place of worship as a place to meet the LORD and not a social club.

62

# Psalm 133

| New American Standard 1995 | Hebrew |
|---|---|
| **Psa. 133:0**  A Song of Ascents, of David.<br><br>**Psa. 133:1**    Behold, how good and how pleasant it is<br>        For *a*brothers to dwell together in unity!<br>2        It is like the precious *a*oil upon the head,<br>        Coming down upon the beard,<br>        *Even* Aaron's beard,<br>        Coming down upon the *b*edge of his robes.<br>3        It is like the *a*dew of *b*Hermon<br>        Coming down upon the *c*mountains of Zion;<br>        For there the LORD *d*commanded the blessing — *e*life forever. | שִׁיר הַמַּעֲלוֹת לְדָוִד הִנֵּה **Psa. 133:1**<br>מַה־טּוֹב וּמַה־נָּעִים שֶׁבֶת אַחִים<br>גַּם־יָחַד : 2 כַּשֶּׁמֶן הַטּוֹב ׀ עַל־<br>הָרֹאשׁ יֹרֵד עַל־הַזָּקָן זְקַן־אַהֲרֹן<br>שֶׁיֹּרֵד עַל־פִּי מִדּוֹתָיו : 3 כְּטַל־<br>חֶרְמוֹן שֶׁיֹּרֵד עַל־הַרְרֵי צִיּוֹן כִּי שָׁם<br>׀ צִוָּה יְהוָה אֶת־הַבְּרָכָה חַיִּים עַד־<br>הָעוֹלָם : |

## References

**Psalm 133:1**
[a]Gen 13:8; Heb 13:1

**Psalm 133:2**
[a]Ex 29:7; 30:25, 30; Lev 8:12
[b]Ex 28:33; 39:24

**Psalm 133:3**
[a]Prov 19:12; Hos 14:5; Mic 5:7
[b]Deut 3:9; 4:48
[c]Ps 48:2; 74:2; 78:68
[d]Lev 25:21; Deut 28:8; Ps 42:8
[e]Ps 21:4

## Targum

**Psa. 133:1** A song that was uttered on the ascents of the abyss. Behold, how good and how pleasant is the dwelling of Zion and Jerusalem, together indeed like two brothers. [2] Like the fine oil that is poured on the head, coming down on the beard, the beard of Aaron, that comes down to the hem of his garments. [3] Like the dew of Hermon that comes down on the mountains of Zion; for there the LORD has commanded the blessing, life forevermore.

## Spiritual Awareness

Introduction

David inherited from Saul a war-torn country. There was a civil war that occurred after Saul's death. Saul had other sons besides Jonathan who claimed the throne. David gathered his men and defeated Saul's remaining sons. David spent a lot of energy to bring the country together. It was Solomon who completed this task. In this Psalm, it is Moses and Aaron who provided the quintessential example of fraternal love. The two brothers were very different in their nature and action. However, they complimented each other and provided the leadership needed for Israel when they left Egypt.

Notes on this Psalm

The psalmist wants people to realize that unity is better than disunity. When a people are unified, they will produce and do wondrous things. When the people are ready to damage each other, that is all they think about. It is also important to accept that people are different. Moses and Aaron were completely different men. However, their differences complimented each other. That is a lesson people need to learn today. The Torah says that a house divided will not stand.

# Psalm 134

| New American Standard 1995 | Hebrew |
| --- | --- |
| **Psa. 134:0**   A Song of Ascents.<br><br>**Psa. 134:1**   Behold, [a]bless the LORD, all [b]servants of the LORD,<br>    Who [1c]serve [d]by night in the house of the LORD!<br>2    [a]Lift   up   your   hands   to   the [b]sanctuary<br>    And bless the LORD.<br>3    May   the   LORD   [a]bless   you   from Zion,<br>    He who [b]made heaven and earth. | שִׁיר הַֽמַּעֲלוֹת הִנֵּה ׀ בָּרְכוּ **Psa. 134:1**<br>אֶת־יְהוָה כָּל־עַבְדֵי יְהוָה<br>הָעֹמְדִים בְּבֵית־יְהוָה בַּלֵּילוֹת׃ 2<br>שְׂאֽוּ־יְדֵכֶם קֹדֶשׁ וּבָרְכוּ אֶת־יְהוָה׃<br>יְבָרֶכְךָ יְהוָה מִצִּיּוֹן עֹשֵׂה שָׁמַיִם 3<br>וָאָרֶץ׃ |

# References


**Psalm 134:1**
[1]Lit *stand*
[a]Ps 103:21
[b]Ps 135:1, 2
[c]Deut 10:8; 1 Chr 23:30; 2 Chr 29:11
[d]1 Chr 9:33


**Psalm 134:2**
[a]Ps 28:2; 1 Tim 2:8
[b]Ps 63:2


**Psalm 134:3**
[a]Ps 128:5
[b]Ps 124:8

## Targum

**Psa. 134:1** A song that was uttered on the ascents of the abyss. Behold, bless the LORD, all servants of the LORD who stand on watch in the sanctuary of the LORD and sing praise at night. [2] Lift up your hands, O priests, on the holy dais, and bless the LORD. [3] The LORD will bless you from Zion, he who made heaven and earth.

## Spiritual Awareness

Introduction

This Psalm is the conclusion of the fifteen Psalms of Ascents, which describes how Israel rises higher and closer to the LORD. The Psalmist shares that the priests who serve the Temple in Zion must spread the blessings from the LORD throughout Israel. After the Temple was destroyed, the people suffered in a dark night of exile. It was the priest's job to inspire the people with a message of Divine encouragement.

Notes on this Psalm

If you are a part of a faith community, ask yourself, is your preaching leader inspiring you to worship, praise and serve the LORD. There are persons who are rabbis and ministers who cannot inspire the people. There are numerous tasks for clergy that those who cannot offer inspiring messages of hope in the not be leading the community. A problem today in the church is that fewer persons want to become pastors. This leaves the denominations with a big problem. How does the leaders get pastors in churches? Unfortunately, today they are forced to assign unqualified persons to these positions. All this does is to reduce the spirituality of the congregation. There are bishops who can inspire the people but are consecrated because they "check boxes" opposed to having the LORD's Shekinah with them. Two problems exist. The first is the lack of persons of God who can inspire the people. The second is the selection of leaders (bishops) by what woke boxes they check off as opposed to their ability to lead. If you have any voice in the decision-making process, it is well pastime to get your voice heard.

# Psalm 135

| New American Standard 1995 | Hebrew |
|---|---|

**Psa. 135:1**　[1][a]Praise [2]the LORD!
Praise the name of the LORD;
Praise *Him,* O [b]servants of the LORD,
[2]　You who stand in the house of the LORD,
In the [a]courts of the house of our God!
[3]　[1]Praise [2]the LORD, for [a]the LORD is good;
[b]Sing praises to His name, [c]for it is lovely.
[4]　For [1]the LORD has [a]chosen Jacob for Himself,
Israel for His [2b]own possession.

**Psa. 135:5**　For I know that [a]the LORD is great
And that our Lord is [b]above all gods.
[6]　[a]Whatever the LORD pleases, He does,
In heaven and in earth, in the seas and in all deeps.
[7]　[1]He [a]causes the [2]vapors to ascend from the ends of the earth;
Who [b]makes lightnings for the rain,
Who [c]brings forth the wind from His treasuries.

**Psa. 135:8**　[1]He [a]smote the firstborn of Egypt,
[2]Both of man and beast.

הַלְלוּ יָהּ ׀ הַלְלוּ אֶת־שֵׁם **Psa. 135:1**
יְהוָה הַלְלוּ עַבְדֵי יְהוָה׃ [2]
שֶׁעֹמְדִים בְּבֵית יְהוָה בְּחַצְרוֹת בֵּית
אֱלֹהֵינוּ׃ [3] הַלְלוּ־יָהּ כִּי־טוֹב יְהוָה
זַמְּרוּ לִשְׁמוֹ כִּי נָעִים׃ [4] כִּי־יַעֲקֹב
בָּחַר לוֹ יָהּ יִשְׂרָאֵל לִסְגֻלָּתוֹ׃ [5] כִּי
אֲנִי יָדַעְתִּי כִּי־גָדוֹל יְהוָה וַאֲדֹנֵינוּ
מִכָּל־אֱלֹהִים׃ [6] כֹּל אֲשֶׁר־חָפֵץ
יְהוָה עָשָׂה בַּשָּׁמַיִם וּבָאָרֶץ בַּיַּמִּים
וְכָל־תְּהוֹמוֹת׃ [7] מַעֲלֶה נְשִׂאִים
מִקְצֵה הָאָרֶץ בְּרָקִים לַמָּטָר עָשָׂה
מוֹצֵא־רוּחַ מֵאוֹצְרוֹתָיו׃ [8] שֶׁהִכָּה
בְּכוֹרֵי מִצְרָיִם מֵאָדָם עַד־בְּהֵמָה׃
[9] שָׁלַח ׀ אֹתוֹת וּמֹפְתִים בְּתוֹכֵכִי
מִצְרַיִם בְּפַרְעֹה וּבְכָל־עֲבָדָיו׃ [10]
שֶׁהִכָּה גּוֹיִם רַבִּים וְהָרַג מְלָכִים
עֲצוּמִים׃ [11] לְסִיחוֹן ׀ מֶלֶךְ הָאֱמֹרִי
וּלְעוֹג מֶלֶךְ הַבָּשָׁן וּלְכֹל מַמְלְכוֹת
כְּנָעַן׃ [12] וְנָתַן אַרְצָם נַחֲלָה נַחֲלָה
לְיִשְׂרָאֵל עַמּוֹ׃ [13] יְהוָה שִׁמְךָ
לְעוֹלָם יְהוָה זִכְרְךָ לְדֹר־וָדֹר׃ [14]
כִּי־יָדִין יְהוָה עַמּוֹ וְעַל־עֲבָדָיו
יִתְנֶחָם׃ [15] עֲצַבֵּי הַגּוֹיִם כֶּסֶף וְזָהָב
מַעֲשֵׂה יְדֵי אָדָם׃ [16] פֶּה־לָהֶם וְלֹא

9 ¹He sent ᵃsigns and wonders into your midst, O Egypt,

Upon ᵇPharaoh and all his servants.

10 ¹ᵃHe ᵇsmote many nations

And slew mighty kings,

11 ᵃSihon, king of the Amorites,

And ᵇOg, king of Bashan,

And ᶜall the kingdoms of Canaan;

12 And He ᵃgave their land as a heritage,

A heritage to Israel His people.

13 Your ᵃname, O LORD, is everlasting,

Your ¹remembrance, O LORD, ²throughout all generations.

14 For the LORD will ᵃjudge His people

And ᵇwill have compassion on His servants.

15 The ᵃidols of the nations are *but* silver and gold,

The work of man's hands.

16 They have mouths, but they do not speak;

They have eyes, but they do not see;

17 They have ears, but they do not hear,

Nor is there any breath at all in their mouths.

18 Those who make them will be like them,

*Yes,* everyone who trusts in them.

**Psa. 135:19** O house of ᵃIsrael, bless the LORD;

O house of Aaron, bless the LORD;

20 O house of Levi, bless the LORD;

יְדַבֵּרוּ עֵינַיִם לָהֶם וְלֹא יִרְאוּ ׃ 17 אָזְנַיִם לָהֶם וְלֹא יַאֲזִינוּ אַף אֵין־ יֶשׁ־רוּחַ בְּפִיהֶם ׃ 18 כְּמוֹהֶם יִהְיוּ עֹשֵׂיהֶם כֹּל אֲשֶׁר־בֹּטֵחַ בָּהֶם ׃ 19 בֵּית יִשְׂרָאֵל בָּרְכוּ אֶת־יְהוָה בֵּית אַהֲרֹן בָּרְכוּ אֶת־יְהוָה ׃ 20 בֵּית הַלֵּוִי בָּרְכוּ אֶת־יְהוָה יִרְאֵי יְהוָה בָּרְכוּ אֶת־יְהוָה ׃ 21 בָּרוּךְ יְהוָה ׀ מִצִּיּוֹן שֹׁכֵן יְרוּשָׁלִָם הַלְלוּ־יָהּ ׃

|  |  |
|---|---|
| You [a]who [1]revere the LORD, bless the LORD.<br>21 Blessed be the LORD [a]from Zion,<br>Who [b]dwells in Jerusalem.<br>[1]Praise [2]the LORD! |  |

# References

**Psalm 135:1**
[1]Or *Hallelujah!*
[2]Heb *YAH*
[a]Ps 113:1
[b]Ps 134:1

**Psalm 135:2**
[a]Ps 92:13; 116:19

**Psalm 135:3**
[1]Or *Hallelujah!*
[2]Heb *YAH*
[a]Ps 100:5; 119:68
[b]Ps 68:4
[c]Ps 147:1

**Psalm 135:4**
[1]Heb *YAH*
[2]Or *special treasure*
[a]Deut 7:6; 10:15; Ps 105:6
[b]Ex 19:5; Mal 3:17; Titus 2:14; 1 Pet 2:9

**Psalm 135:5**
[a]Ps 48:1; 95:3; 145:3
[b]Ps 97:9

**Psalm 135:6**
[a]Ps 115:3

**Psalm 135:7**
[1]Lit *The one who*
[2]I.e. clouds
[a]Jer 10:13; 51:16
[b]Job 28:25, 26; 38:25, 26; Zech 10:1

**Psalm 135:8**
[1]Lit *The one who*
[2]Lit *From man to beast*

[a]Ex 12:12; Ps 78:51; 105:36

**Psalm 135:9**
[1]Lit *The one who*
[a]Ex 7:10; Deut 6:22; Ps 78:43
[b]Ps 136:15

**Psalm 135:10**
[1]Lit *The one who*
[a]Num 21:24; Ps 135:10-12; 136:17-21
[b]Ps 44:2

**Psalm 135:11**
[a]Num 21:21-26; Deut 29:7
[b]Num 21:33-35
[c]Josh 12:7-24

**Psalm 135:12**
[a]Deut 29:8; Ps 78:55; 136:21, 22

**Psalm 135:13**
[1]Or *memorial*
[2]Lit *to*
[a]Ex 3:15; Ps 102:12

**Psalm 135:14**
[a]Deut 32:36; Ps 50:4
[b]Ps 90:13; 106:46

**Psalm 135:15**
[a]Ps 115:4-8; 135:15-18

**Psalm 135:19**
[a]Ps 115:9

**Psalm 135:20**
[1]Lit *fear*
[a]Ps 118:4

**Psalm 135:21**
[1]Or *Hallelujah!*

[2]Heb *YAH*
[a]Ps 128:5; 134:3
[b]Ps 132:14

## Targum

**Psa. 135:1** Hallelujah! Praise the name of the LORD, praise, O servants of the LORD! <sup>2</sup> Who stand in the sanctuary of the LORD, in the courts of the house of our God. <sup>3</sup> Hallelujah! For the LORD is good; sing to his name, for it is pleasant. <sup>4</sup> For the house of Jacob the LORD chose for himself, Israel, for his beloved. <sup>5</sup> For I know, for great is the LORD, and our master over all gods. <sup>6</sup> All that the LORD desires, he has done in heaven and on earth, in the seas and all the deeps. <sup>7</sup> Who brings up clouds from the ends of the earth; he made lightning for the fall of rain, he who brings forth the storm from his storehouses. <sup>8</sup> Who slew the firstborn of Egypt, from man to beast. <sup>9</sup> He sent signs and wonders into your midst, O Egypt, against Pharaoh and all his servants. <sup>10</sup> Who smote many Gentiles and slew mighty kings. <sup>11</sup> Namely, Sihon the Amorite king, and Og, the king of Mathnan, and all the kingdoms of Canaan. <sup>12</sup> And gave their land as an inheritance, an inheritance for Israel his people. <sup>13</sup> O LORD, your name is forever; O LORD, your memorial is for all generations. <sup>14</sup> For the LORD by his word will judge the case of his people, and will turn in his compassion to all his righteous servants. <sup>15</sup> The idols of the Gentiles are silver and gold, the work of the hands of a son of man. <sup>16</sup> They have a mouth, but do not speak; eyes they have, but do not see. <sup>17</sup> They have ears, but do not hear; nostrils, but there is no breath of life in their mouth. <sup>18</sup> Their makers will be like them, all who put their trust in them. <sup>19</sup> house of Israel, bless the LORD! House of Aaron, bless the LORD! <sup>20</sup> House of Levites, bless the LORD! You who fear the LORD, bless the LORD! <sup>21</sup> Blessed is the LORD from Zion, who has made his presence abide in Jerusalem. Hallelujah!

## Spiritual Awareness

Introduction

The Psalmist looks forward to the Messianic era when there will be an unprecedented outpouring of praise to the LORD. Humanity will come to understand that the LORD was in all events.

Notes on this Psalm

This Psalm is a collection of hallelujahs to the LORD for His presence throughout history. Sometimes it is difficult to see the LORD at work in humanity's history because Evil Inclination also exists. The LORD would not cause some of the horror to occur that history talks about. Evil inclination caused the horrors of history. In the days of the Psalmist, it was believed that the LORD caused everything to occur. In modern days scholars have determined that Evil inclination has a lot of influence. The LORD gave humanity freewill. This means that a person can follow Evil Inclination, or the LORD. Those persons who follow the LORD need to show the people who follow Evil Inclination that it is not in their best interest. Evil people need to shed the Klippot and return to the LORD.

# Psalm 136

| New American Standard 1995 | Hebrew |
| --- | --- |

**Psa. 136:1**  *a*Give thanks to the LORD, for *b*He is good,

For  *c*His  lovingkindness  is everlasting.

2  Give thanks to the *a*God of gods,

For  His  lovingkindness  is everlasting.

3  Give thanks to the *a*Lord of lords,

For  His  lovingkindness  is everlasting.

4  To Him who *a*alone does great ¹wonders,

For  His  lovingkindness  is everlasting;

5  To Him who *a*made the heavens ¹*b*with skill,

For  His  lovingkindness  is everlasting;

6  To Him who *a*spread out the earth above the waters,

For  His  lovingkindness  is everlasting;

7  To Him who *a*made *the* great lights,

For  His  lovingkindness  is everlasting:

8  The *a*sun to rule ¹by day,

For  His  lovingkindness  is everlasting,

9  The *a*moon and stars to rule ¹by night,

For  His  lovingkindness  is everlasting.

**Psa. 136:10**  To Him who *a*smote ¹the Egyptians in their firstborn,

---

הוֹדוּ לַיהוָה כִּי־טוֹב כִּי **Psa. 136:1**
לְעוֹלָם חַסְדּוֹ׃ 2 הוֹדוּ לֵאלֹהֵי
הָאֱלֹהִים כִּי לְעוֹלָם חַסְדּוֹ׃ 3 הוֹדוּ
לַאֲדֹנֵי הָאֲדֹנִים כִּי לְעֹלָם חַסְדּוֹ׃ 4
לְעֹשֵׂה נִפְלָאוֹת גְּדֹלוֹת לְבַדּוֹ כִּי
לְעוֹלָם חַסְדּוֹ׃ 5 לְעֹשֵׂה הַשָּׁמַיִם
בִּתְבוּנָה כִּי לְעוֹלָם חַסְדּוֹ׃ 6 לְרֹקַע
הָאָרֶץ עַל־הַמָּיִם כִּי לְעוֹלָם
חַסְדּוֹ׃ 7 לְעֹשֵׂה אוֹרִים גְּדֹלִים כִּי
לְעוֹלָם חַסְדּוֹ׃ 8 אֶת־הַשֶּׁמֶשׁ
לְמֶמְשֶׁלֶת בַּיּוֹם כִּי לְעוֹלָם חַסְדּוֹ׃ 9
אֶת־הַיָּרֵחַ וְכוֹכָבִים לְמֶמְשְׁלוֹת
בַּלָּיְלָה כִּי לְעוֹלָם חַסְדּוֹ׃ 10 לְמַכֵּה
מִצְרַיִם בִּבְכוֹרֵיהֶם כִּי לְעוֹלָם
חַסְדּוֹ׃ 11 וַיּוֹצֵא יִשְׂרָאֵל מִתּוֹכָם כִּי
לְעוֹלָם חַסְדּוֹ׃ 12 בְּיָד חֲזָקָה
וּבִזְרוֹעַ נְטוּיָה כִּי לְעוֹלָם חַסְדּוֹ׃ 13
לְגֹזֵר יַם־סוּף לִגְזָרִים כִּי לְעוֹלָם
חַסְדּוֹ׃ 14 וְהֶעֱבִיר יִשְׂרָאֵל בְּתוֹכוֹ
כִּי לְעוֹלָם חַסְדּוֹ׃ 15 וְנִעֵר פַּרְעֹה
וְחֵילוֹ בְיַם־סוּף כִּי לְעוֹלָם חַסְדּוֹ׃
16 לְמוֹלִיךְ עַמּוֹ בַּמִּדְבָּר כִּי לְעוֹלָם
חַסְדּוֹ׃ 17 לְמַכֵּה מְלָכִים גְּדֹלִים כִּי
לְעוֹלָם חַסְדּוֹ׃ 18 וַיַּהֲרֹג מְלָכִים

For His lovingkindness is everlasting,

**11** And ᵃbrought Israel out from their midst,

For His lovingkindness is everlasting,

**12** With a ᵃstrong hand and an ᵇoutstretched arm,

For His lovingkindness is everlasting.

**13** To Him who ᵃdivided the ¹Red Sea ²asunder,

For His lovingkindness is everlasting,

**14** And ᵃmade Israel pass through the midst of it,

For His lovingkindness is everlasting;

**15** But ᵃHe ¹overthrew Pharaoh and his army in the ²Red Sea,

For His lovingkindness is everlasting.

**16** To Him who ᵃled His people through the wilderness,

For His lovingkindness is everlasting;

**17** To Him who ᵃsmote great kings,

For His lovingkindness is everlasting,

**18** And ᵃslew ¹mighty kings,

For His lovingkindness is everlasting:

**19** ᵃSihon, king of the Amorites,

For His lovingkindness is everlasting,

**20** And ᵃOg, king of Bashan,

For His lovingkindness is everlasting,

**21** And ᵃgave their land as a heritage,

For His lovingkindness is everlasting,

19 אַדִּירִים כִּי לְעוֹלָם חַסְדּוֹ :

לְסִיחוֹן מֶלֶךְ הָאֱמֹרִי כִּי לְעוֹלָם

חַסְדּוֹ : 20 וּלְעוֹג מֶלֶךְ הַבָּשָׁן כִּי

לְעוֹלָם חַסְדּוֹ : 21 וְנָתַן אַרְצָם

לְנַחֲלָה כִּי לְעוֹלָם חַסְדּוֹ : 22 נַחֲלָה

לְיִשְׂרָאֵל עַבְדּוֹ כִּי לְעוֹלָם חַסְדּוֹ :

23 שֶׁבְּשִׁפְלֵנוּ זָכַר לָנוּ כִּי לְעוֹלָם

חַסְדּוֹ : 24 וַיִּפְרְקֵנוּ מִצָּרֵינוּ כִּי

לְעוֹלָם חַסְדּוֹ : 25 נֹתֵן לֶחֶם לְכָל־

בָּשָׂר כִּי לְעוֹלָם חַסְדּוֹ : 26 הוֹדוּ

לְאֵל הַשָּׁמַיִם כִּי לְעוֹלָם חַסְדּוֹ :

[22] Even a heritage to Israel His [a]servant,

For His lovingkindness is everlasting.

**Psa. 136:23** Who [a]remembered us in our low estate,

For His lovingkindness is everlasting,

[24] And has [a]rescued us from our adversaries,

For His lovingkindness is everlasting;

[25] Who [a]gives food to all flesh,

For His lovingkindness is everlasting.

[26] Give thanks to the [a]God of heaven,

For His lovingkindness is everlasting.

# References


**Psalm 136:1**
[a]1 Chr 16:34; Ps 106:1; 107:1; 118:1; Jer 33:11
[b]2 Chr 5:13; 7:3; Ezra 3:11; Ps 100:5
[c]1 Chr 16:41; 2 Chr 20:21; Ps 118:1-4

**Psalm 136:2**
[a]Deut 10:17

**Psalm 136:3**
[a]Deut 10:17

**Psalm 136:4**
[1]I.e. wonderful acts
[a]Deut 6:22; Job 9:10; Ps 72:18

**Psalm 136:5**
[1]Lit *with understanding*
[a]Gen 1:1
[b]Ps 104:24; Prov 3:19; Jer 10:12; 51:15

**Psalm 136:6**
[a]Gen 1:2, 6, 9; Ps 24:2; Is 42:5; 44:24; Jer 10:12

**Psalm 136:7**
[a]Gen 1:14-18; Ps 74:16

**Psalm 136:8**
[1]Or *over the*
[a]Gen 1:16

**Psalm 136:9**
[1]Or *over the*
[a]Gen 1:16

**Psalm 136:10**
[1]Lit *Egypt*
[a]Ex 12:29; Ps 78:51; 135:8

**Psalm 136:11**
*a*Ex 12:51; 13:3; Ps 105:43

**Psalm 136:12**
*a*Ex 6:1; 13:9; 1 Kin 8:42; Neh 1:10; Ps 44:3; Jer 32:21
*b*Ex 6:6; Deut 4:34; 5:15; 7:19; 9:29; 11:2; 2 Kin 17:36; 2 Chr 6:32; Jer 32:17

**Psalm 136:13**
[1]Lit *Sea of Reeds*
[2]Lit *in parts*
*a*Ex 14:21; Ps 66:6; 78:13

**Psalm 136:14**
*a*Ex 14:22; Ps 106:9

**Psalm 136:15**
[1]Lit *shook off*
[2]Lit *Sea of Reeds*
*a*Ex 14:27; Ps 78:53; 106:11

**Psalm 136:16**
*a*Ex 13:18; 15:22; Deut 8:15; Ps 78:52

**Psalm 136:17**
*a*Ps 135:10-12; 136:17-22

**Psalm 136:18**
[1]Lit *majestic*
*a*Deut 29:7

**Psalm 136:19**
*a*Num 21:21-24

**Psalm 136:20**
*a*Num 21:33-35

**Psalm 136:21**
*a*Josh 12:1

**Psalm 136:22**
*a*Ps 105:6; Is 41:8; 44:1; 45:4

**Psalm 136:23**
*a*Ps 9:12; 103:14; 106:45

**Psalm 136:24**
*a*Judg 6:9; Neh 9:28; Ps 107:2

**Psalm 136:25**
*a*Ps 104:27; 145:15

**Psalm 136:26**
*a*Gen 24:3, 7; 2 Chr 36:23; Ezra 1:2; 5:11; Neh 1:4

## Targum

**Psa. 136:1** Sing praise in the presence of the LORD, for he is good, for his goodness is forever. [2] Sing praise to the God of gods, for his goodness is forever. [3] Sing praise to the Lord of lords, for his goodness is forever. [4] To him who did great wonders by himself, for his goodness is forever. [5] To him who made the heavens by insight, for his goodness is forever. [6] To him who made firm the earth on the waters, for his goodness is forever. [7] To him who made great lights, for his goodness is forever. [8] The sun to rule by day, for his goodness is forever. [9] The moon and stars to rule by night, for his goodness is forever. [10] To him who smites the Egyptians with plagues, killing the firstborn, for his goodness is forever. [11] And brought out Israel redeemed from among them, for his goodness is forever. [12] With a mighty hand and upraised arm, for his goodness is forever. [13] To him who split the Sea of Reeds into pieces, for his goodness is forever. [14] And made Israel cross over in the middle of it, for his goodness is forever. [15] And choked Pharaoh and his forces in the Sea of Reeds, for his goodness is forever. [16] To him who led his people in the wilderness, for his goodness is forever. [17] To him who smites great kings, for his goodness is forever. [18] And slew proud kings, for his goodness is forever. [19] Namely, Sihon the Amorite king, for his goodness is forever. [20] And Og, king of Mathnan, for his goodness is forever. [21] And gave their land as an inheritance, for his goodness is forever. [22] An inheritance to Israel his servant, for his goodness is forever. [23] In our humiliation he remembered his covenant with us, for his goodness is forever. [24] And redeemed us from our oppressors, for his goodness is forever. [25] Who gives his food to all flesh, for his goodness is forever. [26] Sing praise to the God of heaven, for his goodness is forever.

## Spiritual Awareness

Introduction

This Psalm is twenty-six verses. This corresponds to the numerical value of the Four-letter name of the LORD. This designates that the LORD is the creator of Heaven and Earth. The Psalm is a collection of events from creation to Israel's conquest of Canaan.

Notes on this Psalm

Verse one – the Psalmist starts by acknowledging the LORD's love through the Sefirah Chesed. The Psalmist does this for all the verses of the Psalm.

**Acknowledge it to God that He is good, that His loving-kindness from the Sefirah Chesed endures forever.**

The message is that the loving-kindness of the LORD comes from the Sefirah Chesed and it will last forever.

# Psalm 137

| New American Standard 1995 | Hebrew |
| --- | --- |
| **Psa. 137:1**  By the [a]rivers of Babylon, There we sat down and [b]wept, When we remembered Zion.<br>2  Upon the [1a]willows in the midst of it<br>We [b]hung our [2]harps.<br>3  For there our captors [1a]demanded of us [2]songs,<br>And [b]our tormentors mirth, *saying,*<br>"Sing us one of the songs of Zion."<br><br>**Psa. 137:4**  How can we sing [a]the LORD'S song<br>In a foreign land?<br>5  If I [a]forget you, O Jerusalem,<br>May my right hand [1]forget *her skill.*<br>6  May my [a]tongue cling to the roof of my mouth<br>If I do not remember you,<br>If I do not [1b]exalt Jerusalem<br>Above my chief joy.<br><br>**Psa. 137:7**  Remember, O LORD, against the sons of [a]Edom<br>The day of Jerusalem,<br>Who said, "Raze it, raze it<br>[b]To its very foundation."<br>8  O daughter of Babylon, you [1a]devastated one,<br>How blessed will be the one who [b]repays you<br>With [2]the recompense with which you have repaid us. | עַל נַהֲרוֹת ׀ בָּבֶל שָׁם **Psa. 137:1**<br>יָשַׁבְנוּ גַּם־בָּכִינוּ בְּזָכְרֵנוּ אֶת־<br>צִיּוֹן׃ 2 עַל־עֲרָבִים בְּתוֹכָהּ<br>תָּלִינוּ כִּנֹּרוֹתֵינוּ׃ 3 כִּי שָׁם<br>שְׁאֵלוּנוּ שׁוֹבֵינוּ דִּבְרֵי־שִׁיר<br>וְתוֹלָלֵינוּ שִׂמְחָה שִׁירוּ לָנוּ<br>מִשִּׁיר צִיּוֹן׃ 4 אֵיךְ נָשִׁיר אֶת־<br>שִׁיר־יְהוָה עַל אַדְמַת נֵכָר׃ 5<br>אִם־אֶשְׁכָּחֵךְ יְרוּשָׁלָ͏ִם תִּשְׁכַּח<br>יְמִינִי׃ 6 תִּדְבַּק־לְשׁוֹנִי ׀ לְחִכִּי<br>אִם־לֹא אֶזְכְּרֵכִי אִם־לֹא<br>אַעֲלֶה אֶת־יְרוּשָׁלַ͏ִם עַל רֹאשׁ<br>שִׂמְחָתִי׃ 7 זְכֹר יְהוָה ׀ לִבְנֵי<br>אֱדוֹם אֵת יוֹם יְרוּשָׁלָ͏ִם<br>הָאֹמְרִים עָרוּ ׀ עָרוּ עַד הַיְסוֹד<br>בָּהּ׃ 8 בַּת־בָּבֶל הַשְּׁדוּדָה<br>אַשְׁרֵי שֶׁיְשַׁלֶּם־לָךְ אֶת־גְּמוּלֵךְ<br>שֶׁגָּמַלְתְּ לָנוּ׃ 9 אַשְׁרֵי ׀ שֶׁיֹּאחֵז<br>וְנִפֵּץ אֶת־עֹלָלַיִךְ אֶל־הַסָּלַע׃ |

<table>
<tr><td>[9]     How blessed will be the one who seizes and [a]dashes your little ones<br>       Against the rock.</td><td></td></tr>
</table>

# References

**Psalm 137:1**
[a]Ezek 1:1, 3
[b]Neh 1:4

**Psalm 137:2**
[1]Or *poplars*
[2]Lit *lyres*
[a]Lev 23:40; Is 44:4
[b]Job 30:31; Is 24:8; Ezek 26:13

**Psalm 137:3**
[1]Lit *asked*
[2]Lit *words of song*
[a]Ps 80:6
[b]Is 49:17

**Psalm 137:4**
[a]2 Chr 29:27; Neh 12:46

**Psalm 137:5**
[1]I.e. become lame
[a]Is 65:11

**Psalm 137:6**
[1]Lit *cause to ascend*
[a]Job 29:10; Ps 22:15; Ezek 3:26
[b]Neh 2:3

**Psalm 137:7**
[a]Ps 83:4-8; Is 34:5, 6; Jer 49:7-22; Lam 4:21; Ezek 25:12-14; 35:2; Amos 1:11; Obad 10-14
[b]Ps 74:7; Hab 3:13

**Psalm 137:8**
[1]Or *devastator*
[2]Lit *your recompense*
[a]Is 13:1-22; 47:1-15; Jer 25:12; 50:1-46; 51:1-64

[b]Jer 50:15; 51:24, 35, 36, 49; Rev 18:6

**Psalm 137:9**
[a]2 Kin 8:12; Is 13:16; Hos 13:16; Nah 3:10

## Targum

**Psa. 137:1** By the rivers of Babylon, there we sat down, also we wept, as we were remembering Zion. **2** On the willows in her midst we hung our harps. **3** For there the Babylonians who captured us asked us to utter the words of songs; and our despoilers, because of [their] joy, were saying, "Sing for us some of the songs you used to utter in Zion." **4** At once the Levites cut off their thumbs with their teeth, and say, "How can we sing the praise of the LORD on profane land?" **5** The voice of the holy spirit replies and says, "If I forget you, O Jerusalem, I will forget my right hand." **6** My tongue will cleave to my palate, if I will not remember you; if I will not elevate the memory of Jerusalem above the principal joy of my temple. **7** Said Michael, prince of Jerusalem, "Remember, O LORD, the people of Edom, who laid waste Jerusalem, who say, 'Destroy, destroy, to the foundations of it.' " **8** Said Gabriel, prince of Zion to the despoiling Babylonian mother, "Happy he who gives back to you evil for what you did to us." **9** Happy he who takes and smashes your children on a rock.

## Spiritual Awareness

### Introduction

This Psalm conveys the intense mourning of a once joyous nation shrouded in the gloom of being in exile from their homeland. The people remembered the glory of Mount Zion and sadden because of its destruction at the hands of the Babylonians. There is a custom for the bridegroom to recite this verse under the wedding canopy as he awaits his bride, to fulfill the Jew's eternal vow not to fail to elevate Jerusalem above his foremost joy (verse six).

### Notes on this Psalm

Verse nine is one that is usually misunderstood. The author did not want to see children's heads smashed against rocks. This was a known curse spoken against an enemy. It is actually a request to the LORD that the enemy be destroyed because the enemy attacked the LORD's people. This Psalm should remind the reader that anything that the LORD gives can be taken away. Why would the LORD take a gift away? As the people of Judah discovered when they violated the LORD's Law, especially pagan worship in the LORD's Temple, then the LORD will react. In this case, He removed his protection from Judah and the Babylonians conquered it. Always remember that everything one has is from the LORD.

# Psalm 138

| New American Standard 1995 | Hebrew |
| --- | --- |
| **Psa. 138:0**  *A Psalm* of David. | **Psa. 138:1** לְדָוִד ׀ אוֹדְךָ בְכָל־לִבִּי נֶגֶד |
| **Psa. 138:1**  *a*I will give You thanks with all my heart; | אֱלֹהִים אֲזַמְּרֶךָּ : 2 אֶשְׁתַּחֲוֶה אֶל־הֵיכַל |
| I will sing praises to You before the *b*gods. | קָדְשְׁךָ וְאוֹדֶה אֶת־שְׁמֶךָ עַל־חַסְדְּךָ וְעַל־ |
| 2 I will bow down *a*toward Your holy temple | אֲמִתֶּךָ כִּי־הִגְדַּלְתָּ עַל־כָּל־שִׁמְךָ אִמְרָתֶךָ : 3 |
| And *b*give thanks to Your name for Your lovingkindness and Your [1]truth; | בְּיוֹם קָרָאתִי וַתַּעֲנֵנִי תַּרְהִבֵנִי בְנַפְשִׁי עֹז : 4 |
| For You have *c*magnified Your [2]word [3]according to all Your name. | יוֹדוּךָ יְהוָה כָּל־מַלְכֵי־אָרֶץ כִּי שָׁמְעוּ אִמְרֵי־ |
| 3 On the day I *a*called, You answered me; | פִיךָ : 5 וְיָשִׁירוּ בְּדַרְכֵי יְהוָה כִּי גָדוֹל כְּבוֹד |
| You made me bold with *b*strength in my soul. | יְהוָה : 6 כִּי־רָם יְהוָה וְשָׁפָל יִרְאֶה וְגָבֹהַּ |
| **Psa. 138:4**  *a*All the kings of the earth will give thanks to You, O LORD, | מִמֶּרְחָק יְיֵדָע : 7 אִם־אֵלֵךְ ׀ בְּקֶרֶב צָרָה |
| When they have heard the words of Your mouth. | תְּחַיֵּנִי עַל אַף אֹיְבַי תִּשְׁלַח יָדֶךָ וְתוֹשִׁיעֵנִי |
| 5 And they will *a*sing of the ways of the LORD, | יְמִינֶךָ : 8 יְהוָה יִגְמֹר בַּעֲדִי יְהוָה חַסְדְּךָ |
| For *b*great is the glory of the LORD. | לְעוֹלָם מַעֲשֵׂי יָדֶיךָ אַל־תֶּרֶף : |
| 6 For *a*though the LORD is exalted, Yet He *b*regards the lowly, | |
| But the *c*haughty He knows from afar. | |
| **Psa. 138:7**  Though I *a*walk in the midst of trouble, You will [1]*b*revive me; | |
| You will *c*stretch forth Your hand against the wrath of my enemies, | |
| And Your right hand will *d*save me. | |

| | |
|---|---|
| 8    The LORD will [a]accomplish what concerns me;<br>    Your [b]lovingkindness, O LORD, is everlasting;<br>    [c]Do not forsake the [d]works of Your hands. | |

# References

**Psalm 138:1**
[a]Ps 111:1
[b]Ps 95:3; 96:4; 97:7

**Psalm 138:2**
[1]Or *faithfulness*
[2]Or *promise*
[3]Or *together with*
[a]1 Kin 8:29; Ps 5:7; 28:2
[b]Ps 140:13
[c]Is 42:21

**Psalm 138:3**
[a]Ps 118:5
[b]Ps 28:7; 46:1

**Psalm 138:4**
[a]Ps 72:11; 102:15

**Psalm 138:5**
[a]Ps 145:7
[b]Ps 21:5

**Psalm 138:6**
[a]Ps 113:4-7
[b]Prov 3:34; Is 57:15; Luke 1:48; James 4:6; 1 Pet 5:5
[c]Ps 40:4; 101:5

**Psalm 138:7**
[1]Or *keep me alive*
[a]Ps 23:4; 143:11
[b]Ezra 9:8, 9; Ps 71:20; Is 57:15
[c]Ex 7:5; 15:12; Is 5:25; Jer 51:25; Ezek 6:14; 25:13
[d]Ps 20:6; 60:5

**Psalm 138:8**
[a]Ps 57:2; Phil 1:6
[b]Ps 136:1
[c]Job 10:8; Ps 27:9; 71:9; 119:8

<sup>d</sup>Job 10:3; 14:15; Ps 100:3

## Targum

**Psa. 138:1** Composed by David. I will give thanks in your presence, O LORD, with all my heart; before the judges I will sing to you. ² I will bow down before your temple, and I will confess your name, because of your goodness and because of your truth; for you have magnified over every name of yours the utterance of your praise. ³ In the day that I call, answer me; you have magnified strength in my soul. ⁴ All the kings of the earth will give thanks in your presence, O LORD, for they have heard the utterance of your praise. ⁵ And they will sing praise on the pathways of the LORD, for great is the glory of the LORD. ⁶ For exalted is the LORD, but he will look on the humble for good; but he will humble the proud from heaven afar. ⁷ If I walk in the midst of trouble, you will keep me alive; you will stretch forth your hand against the nostrils of my enemies to destroy them, and your right hand will redeem me. ⁸ The LORD will pay them back evil on my account; O LORD, your goodness is forever, you will not forsake the works of your hands.

## Spiritual Awareness

Introduction

This Psalm captures the triumphant spirits that will pervade the nation when the Messianic age comes. The enemies of Israel will be removed by the LORD.

Notes on this Psalm

Imagine a world where every person lives by the Laws of the LORD. Peace and tranquility would be the mainstay of the people. That day will come when the Messiah comes, and the Messianic age begins. The author calls upon the Sefirah Chesed to send the LORD's lovingkindness to start the Messianic age.

# Psalm 139

| New American Standard 1995 | Hebrew |
| --- | --- |

**Psa. 139:0**  For the choir director. A Psalm of David.

**Psa. 139:1**  O LORD, You have [a]searched me and known *me*.
2    You [a]know [1]when I sit down and [2]when I rise up;
You [b]understand my thought from afar.
3    You [1a]scrutinize my [2]path and my lying down,
And are intimately acquainted with all my ways.
4    [1]Even before there is a word on my tongue,
Behold, O LORD, You [a]know it all.
5    You have [a]enclosed me behind and before,
And [b]laid Your hand upon me.
6    *Such* [a]knowledge is [b]too wonderful for me;
It is *too* high, I cannot attain to it.

**Psa. 139:7**  [a]Where can I go from Your Spirit?
Or where can I flee from Your presence?
8    [a]If I ascend to heaven, You are there;
If I make my bed in [1]Sheol, behold, [b]You are there.
9    If I take the wings of the dawn,
If I dwell in the remotest part of the sea,

לַמְנַצֵּחַ לְדָוִד מִזְמוֹר יְהוָה **Psa. 139:1**
חֲקַרְתַּנִי וַתֵּדָע׃ ² אַתָּה יָדַעְתָּ
שִׁבְתִּי וְקוּמִי בַּנְתָּה לְרֵעִי מֵרָחוֹק׃
³ אָרְחִי וְרִבְעִי זֵרִיתָ וְכָל־דְּרָכַי
הִסְכַּנְתָּה׃ ⁴ כִּי אֵין מִלָּה בִּלְשׁוֹנִי
הֵן יְהוָה יָדַעְתָּ כֻלָּהּ׃ ⁵ אָחוֹר
וָקֶדֶם צַרְתָּנִי וַתָּשֶׁת עָלַי כַּפֶּכָה׃ ⁶
פְּלִאיָה [פְּלִיאָה] דַעַת מִמֶּנִּי
נִשְׂגְּבָה לֹא־אוּכַל לָהּ׃ ⁷ אָנָה אֵלֵךְ
מֵרוּחֶךָ וְאָנָה מִפָּנֶיךָ אֶבְרָח׃ ⁸
אִם־אֶסַּק שָׁמַיִם שָׁם אָתָּה וְאַצִּיעָה
שְּׁאוֹל הִנֶּךָּ׃ ⁹ אֶשָּׂא כַנְפֵי־שָׁחַר
אֶשְׁכְּנָה בְּאַחֲרִית יָם׃ ¹⁰ גַּם־שָׁם
יָדְךָ תַנְחֵנִי וְתֹאחֲזֵנִי יְמִינֶךָ׃ ¹¹
וָאֹמַר אַךְ־חֹשֶׁךְ יְשׁוּפֵנִי וְלַיְלָה אוֹר
בַּעֲדֵנִי׃ ¹² גַּם־חֹשֶׁךְ לֹא־יַחְשִׁיךְ
מִמֶּךָ וְלַיְלָה כַּיּוֹם יָאִיר כַּחֲשֵׁיכָה
כָּאוֹרָה׃ ¹³ כִּי־אַתָּה קָנִיתָ כִלְיֹתָי
תְּסֻכֵּנִי בְּבֶטֶן אִמִּי׃ ¹⁴ אוֹדְךָ עַל כִּי
נוֹרָאוֹת נִפְלֵיתִי נִפְלָאִים מַעֲשֶׂיךָ
וְנַפְשִׁי יֹדַעַת מְאֹד׃ ¹⁵ לֹא־נִכְחַד
עָצְמִי מִמֶּךָּ אֲשֶׁר־עֻשֵּׂיתִי בַסֵּתֶר
רֻקַּמְתִּי בְּתַחְתִּיּוֹת אָרֶץ׃ ¹⁶ גָּלְמִי |
רָאוּ עֵינֶיךָ וְעַל־סִפְרְךָ כֻּלָּם

10 Even there Your hand will [a]lead me,

And Your right hand will lay hold of me.

11 If I say, "Surely the [a]darkness will [1]overwhelm me,

And the light around me will be night,"

12 Even the [a]darkness is not dark [1]to You,

And the night is as bright as the day.

[b]Darkness and light are alike *to You.*

**Psa. 139:13** For You [a]formed my [1]inward parts;

You [b]wove me in my mother's womb.

14 I will give thanks to You, for [1]I am fearfully and wonderfully made;

[a]Wonderful are Your works,

And my soul knows it very well.

15 My [1a]frame was not hidden from You,

When I was made in secret,

*And* skillfully wrought in the [b]depths of the earth;

16 Your [a]eyes have seen my unformed substance;

And in [b]Your book were all written

The [c]days that were ordained *for me,*

When as yet there was not one of them.

**Psa. 139:17** How precious also are Your [a]thoughts to me, O God!

How vast is the sum of them!

18 If I should count them, they would [a]outnumber the sand.

When [b]I awake, I am still with You.

יִכָּתֵבוּ יָמִים יֻצָּרוּ וְלֹא [וְ][לוֹ]
אֶחָד בָּהֶם : וְלִי מַה־יָּקְרוּ רֵעֶיךָ 17
אֵל מֶה עָצְמוּ רָאשֵׁיהֶם : אֶסְפְּרֵם 18
מֵחוֹל יִרְבּוּן הֱקִיצֹתִי וְעוֹדִי עִמָּךְ :
אִם־תִּקְטֹל אֱלוֹהַּ וְרֶשַׁע וְאַנְשֵׁי 19
דָמִים סוּרוּ מֶנִּי : אֲשֶׁר יֹאמְרֻךָ 20
לִמְזִמָּה נָשֻׂא לַשָּׁוְא עָרֶיךָ : 21
הֲלוֹא־מְשַׂנְאֶיךָ יְהוָה אֶשְׂנָא
וּבִתְקוֹמְמֶיךָ אֶתְקוֹטָט : תַּכְלִית 22
שִׂנְאָה שְׂנֵאתִים לְאוֹיְבִים הָיוּ לִי : 23
חָקְרֵנִי אֵל וְדַע לְבָבִי בְּחָנֵנִי וְדַע
שַׂרְעַפָּי : וּרְאֵה אִם־דֶּרֶךְ־עֹצֶב 24
בִּי וּנְחֵנִי בְּדֶרֶךְ עוֹלָם :

**Psa. 139:19**    O that You would *a*slay the wicked, O God;

*b*Depart from me, therefore, *c*men of bloodshed.

20    For they *a*speak [1]against You wickedly,

And Your enemies [2b]take *Your name* in vain.

21    Do I not *a*hate those who hate You, O LORD?

And do I not *b*loathe those who rise up against You?

22    I hate them with the utmost hatred;

They have become my enemies.


**Psa. 139:23**    *a*Search me, O God, and know my heart;

*b*Try me and know my anxious thoughts;

24    And see if there be any [1a]hurtful way in me,

And *b*lead me in the *c*everlasting way.

## References

**Psalm 139:1**
[a]Ps 17:3; 44:21; Jer 12:3

**Psalm 139:2**
[1]Lit *my sitting*
[2]Lit *my rising*
[a]2 Kin 19:27
[b]Ps 94:11; Is 66:18; Matt 9:4

**Psalm 139:3**
[1]Lit *winnow*
[2]Or *journeying*
[a]Job 14:16; 31:4

**Psalm 139:4**
[1]Lit *For there is not*
[a]Heb 4:13

**Psalm 139:5**
[a]Ps 34:7; 125:2
[b]Job 9:33

**Psalm 139:6**
[a]Rom 11:33
[b]Job 42:3

**Psalm 139:7**
[a]Jer 23:24

**Psalm 139:8**
[1]I.e. the nether world
[a]Amos 9:2-4
[b]Job 26:6; Prov 15:11

**Psalm 139:10**
[a]Ps 23:2, 3

**Psalm 139:11**

[1]Lit *bruise;* some commentators read *cover*
[q]Job 22:13

**Psalm 139:12**
[1]Lit *from*
[a]Job 34:22; Dan 2:22
[b]1 John 1:5

**Psalm 139:13**
[1]Lit *kidneys*
[a]Ps 119:73; Is 44:24
[b]Job 10:11

**Psalm 139:14**
[1]Some ancient versions read *You are fearfully wonderful*
[a]Ps 40:5

**Psalm 139:15**
[1]Lit *bones were*
[a]Job 10:8-10; Eccl 11:5
[b]Ps 63:9

**Psalm 139:16**
[a]Job 10:8-10; Eccl 11:5
[b]Ps 56:8
[c]Job 14:5

**Psalm 139:17**
[a]Ps 40:5; 92:5

**Psalm 139:18**
[a]Ps 40:5
[b]Ps 3:5

**Psalm 139:19**
[a]Is 11:4
[b]Ps 6:8; 119:115
[c]Ps 5:6; 26:9

**Psalm 139:20**
[1]Or *of*

[2]Some mss read *lift themselves up* against You
[a]Jude 15
[b]Ex 20:7; Deut 5:11

**Psalm 139:21**
[a]2 Chr 19:2; Ps 26:5; 31:6
[b]Ps 119:158

**Psalm 139:23**
[a]Job 31:6; Ps 26:2
[b]Ps 7:9; Prov 17:3; Jer 11:20; 1 Thess 2:4

**Psalm 139:24**
[1]Lit *way of pain*
[a]Ps 146:9; Prov 15:9; 28:10; Jer 25:5; 36:3
[b]Ps 5:8; 143:10
[c]Ps 16:11

## Targum

**Psa. 139:1** For praise, composed by David, a psalm. O LORD, you have searched me out and known me. [2] It is manifest before you when I sit down to study the Torah, and when I rise up to go to war; you understand my fellowship in your congregation from a people afar off. [3] Now when I walk in the road or when I recline to study the Torah, you have become a stranger; and you have made all my ways dangerous. [4] And when there is no speech on my tongue, behold, O LORD, you know the thought of my heart completely. [5] From behind me and in front of me you have confined me, and you have inflicted on me the blow of your hand. [6] It is hidden from my knowing; it is too mighty, I am not capable of it. [7] Where will I go from the presence of your storm-wind? And where shall I flee from your presence? [8] If I go up to the heavens, you are there; and if I lower myself to Sheol, behold, there is your word. [9] I will lift up the fringes of sunrise, I will abide at the ends of the sea. [10] Also there your hand will guide me, and your right hand will seize me. [11] And I said, "Truly, darkness will blind me, and the night will become dark for my sake." [12] Also the darkness will not be too dark for your word, and the night, like day, will give light; like darkness, like light – they are equal. [13] For you have created my kidneys; you established me in the belly of my mother. [14] I will give you thanks, for you have miraculously done awesome things; your works are wonderful, and my soul knows it well. [15] My self is not hidden from you, for I was made in secret, I was formed in the belly of my mother. [16] Your eyes see my body; and in the book of your remembrance all my days were written on the day the world was created; in the beginning all creatures were created but not on a single day among them. [17] And how precious to me are those who love you, the righteous, O God; and how mighty have their scholars become! [18] I will number them in this age: they will be more numerous than sand; I awake in the age to come and still I am with you. [19] If you slay, O God, the wicked man, [then] men who are worthy of the judgment of death will depart from me. [20] Who will swear in your name for deception, taking an oath in vain, your enemies. [21] Do I not hate all those who hate you, O LORD? And when they rise against you, I am incensed. [22] I hate them to the destruction of hatred; they have become enemies to me. [23] Search me out, O God, and know my thoughts; examine me and know my thinking. [24] And see if any way of error is in me; and guide me in the path of those eternally upright.

## Spiritual Awareness

Introduction

The sage Ibn Ezra described this Psalm as an extraordinary lesson on the ways of the LORD. This is the only Psalm which examines the roots and reasons for creation so intimately. As every new generation enters their stage of history, it follows an ancient script, and a predetermined Divine drama unfolds. Humanity was freewill to choose which direction it will go. This is a paradox that the rabbis have debated for centuries. If freewill exists, then a predetermined drama cannot exist. Only the LORD can explain how these two items are in balance.

Superscript

The author calls upon the Sefirah Netzach for victory.

**To Him who grants victory, by David, a psalm.**

Notes on this Psalm

Predetermination is an interesting topic to discuss. On one hand, if this exists then humanity is a puppet of the LORD as He pulls the strings. Freewill allows humanity to create its own destiny. This paradox is debated in many writings and has been debated by sages and rabbis. Does the LORD influence daily life on Earth? There are people who believe that the LORD created the Earth and humanity but then left to watch what would happen. A problem with this idea is that it is clear there are historical events where the LORD has stepped in. For example, the LORD's work was seen at the Exodus and the Red Sea. The LORD became known to Israel when it camped at the base of Mount Sinai. There is a Midrash that says that the LORD allowed Adam to see the future. Adam saw what was to happen to King David and gave him 25 years of his life. Adam lived to 975 years instead of 1000 years. This Midrash comes out on the side of predetermination. But if this exists, then why would the LORD allow the sins that caused the destruction of the Temple to occur? Certainly, the LORD would have been able to stop that from happening.

This debate will continue through the centuries until humanity dies out. This is a secret of existence that one will discover the answer to when one returns to the Lower Waters of Heaven. Perhaps we will discover that the LORD's system was to allow freewill that would not affect the Divine history of humanity.

# Psalm 140

| New American Standard 1995 | Hebrew |
|---|---|
| | |

**Psa. 140:0**  For the choir director. A Psalm of David.

**Psa. 140:1**  <sup>a</sup>Rescue me, O LORD, from evil men;
　　Preserve me from <sup>b</sup>violent men
2　　Who <sup>a</sup>devise evil things in *their* hearts;
　　They <sup>b</sup>continually stir up wars.
3　　They <sup>a</sup>sharpen their tongues as a serpent;
　　<sup>b</sup>Poison of a viper is under their lips.  <sup>1</sup>Selah.

**Psa. 140:4**  <sup>a</sup>Keep me, O LORD, from the hands of the wicked;
　　<sup>b</sup>Preserve me from violent men
　　Who have <sup>1</sup>purposed to <sup>2c</sup>trip up my feet.
5　　The proud have <sup>a</sup>hidden a trap for me, and cords;
　　They have spread a <sup>b</sup>net by the <sup>1</sup>wayside;
　　They have set <sup>c</sup>snares for me. Selah.

**Psa. 140:6**  I <sup>a</sup>said to the LORD, "You are my God;
　　<sup>b</sup>Give ear, O LORD, to the <sup>c</sup>voice of my supplications.
7　　"O <sup>1</sup>GOD the Lord, <sup>a</sup>the strength of my salvation,
　　You have <sup>b</sup>covered my head in the day of <sup>2</sup>battle.

**Psa. 140:1** לַמְנַצֵּחַ מִזְמוֹר לְדָוִד ׃ 2

חַלְּצֵנִי יְהוָה מֵאָדָם רָע מֵאִישׁ

חֲמָסִים תִּנְצְרֵנִי ׃ 3 אֲשֶׁר חָשְׁבוּ

רָעוֹת בְּלֵב כָּל־יוֹם יָגוּרוּ

מִלְחָמוֹת ׃ 4 שָׁנְנוּ לְשׁוֹנָם כְּמוֹ־נָחָשׁ

חֲמַת עַכְשׁוּב תַּחַת שְׂפָתֵימוֹ סֶלָה ׃

5 שָׁמְרֵנִי יְהוָה מִידֵי רָשָׁע מֵאִישׁ

חֲמָסִים תִּנְצְרֵנִי אֲשֶׁר חָשְׁבוּ

לִדְחוֹת פְּעָמָי ׃ 6 טָמְנוּ־גֵאִים וּפַח

לִי וַחֲבָלִים פָּרְשׂוּ רֶשֶׁת לְיַד־מַעְגָּל

מֹקְשִׁים שָׁתוּ־לִי סֶלָה ׃ 7 אָמַרְתִּי

לַיהוָה אֵלִי אָתָּה הַאֲזִינָה יְהוָה

קוֹל תַּחֲנוּנָי ׃ 8 יְהוִה אֲדֹנָי עֹז

יְשׁוּעָתִי סַכֹּתָה לְרֹאשִׁי בְּיוֹם נָשֶׁק ׃

9 אַל־תִּתֵּן יְהוָה מַאֲוַיֵּי רָשָׁע זְמָמוֹ

אַל־תָּפֵק יָרוּמוּ סֶלָה ׃ 10 רֹאשׁ

מְסִבָּי עֲמַל שְׂפָתֵימוֹ יְכַסּוּמוֹ

[יְכַסֵּמוֹ] ׃ 11 יִמּוֹטוּ [יִמּוֹטוּ] עֲלֵיהֶם

גֶּחָלִים בָּאֵשׁ יַפִּלֵם בְּמַהֲמֹרוֹת בַּל־

יָקוּמוּ ׃ 12 אִישׁ לָשׁוֹן בַּל־יִכּוֹן

בָּאָרֶץ אִישׁ־חָמָס רָע יְצוּדֶנּוּ

לְמַדְחֵפֹת ׃ 13 יָדַעְתָּ [יָדַעְתִּי] כִּי־

יַעֲשֶׂה יְהוָה דִּין עָנִי מִשְׁפַּט

8    "Do not grant, O LORD, the
*desires of the wicked;
    Do not promote *his *evil* device,
*that* they *not* be exalted.  Selah.

**Psa. 140:9**    "As for the head of those
who surround me,
    May the *mischief of their lips
cover them.
10    "May *burning coals fall upon
them;
    May they be *cast into the fire,
    Into ¹deep pits from which they
*cannot rise.
11    "May a ¹slanderer not be
established in the earth;
    *May evil hunt the violent man
²speedily."

**Psa. 140:12**        I know that the
LORD will *maintain the cause of the
afflicted
    And *justice for the poor.
13    Surely the *righteous will give
thanks to Your name;
    The *upright  will  dwell  in  Your
presence.

אֲבִינֶים : ‏14 אַ֤ךְ צַדִּיקִים יוֹד֣וּ
לִשְׁמֶ֑ךָ יֵשְׁב֥וּ יְ֜שָׁרִ֗ים אֶת־פָּנֶֽיךָ :

# References

**Psalm 140:1**
[a]Ps 17:13; 59:2; 71:4
[b]Ps 18:48; 86:14; 140:11

**Psalm 140:2**
[a]Ps 7:14; 36:4; 52:2; Prov 6:14; Is 59:4; Hos 7:15
[b]Ps 56:6

**Psalm 140:3**
[1]*Selah* may mean: *Pause, Crescendo* or *Musical interlude*
[a]Ps 57:4; 64:3
[b]Ps 58:4; Rom 3:13; James 3:8

**Psalm 140:4**
[1]Or *devised*
[2]Lit *push violently*
[a]Ps 71:4
[b]Ps 140:1
[c]Ps 36:11

**Psalm 140:5**
[1]Lit *track*
[a]Job 18:9; Ps 35:7; 141:9; 142:3
[b]Ps 31:4; 57:6; Lam 1:13
[c]Ps 141:9; Is 8:14; Amos 3:5

**Psalm 140:6**
[a]Ps 16:2; 31:14
[b]Ps 143:1
[c]Ps 116:1; 130:2

**Psalm 140:7**
[1]Heb *YHWH,* usually rendered *LORD*
[2]Lit *weapons*
[a]Ps 28:8; 118:14
[b]Ps 144:10

**Psalm 140:8**

[a]Ps 112:10
[b]Esth 9:25; Ps 10:2, 3

**Psalm 140:9**
[a]Ps 7:16; Prov 18:7

**Psalm 140:10**
[1]Lit *watery*
[a]Ps 11:6
[b]Ps 21:9; Matt 3:10
[c]Ps 36:12

**Psalm 140:11**
[1]Lit *man of tongue*
[2]Lit *thrust upon thrust*
[a]Ps 34:21

**Psalm 140:12**
[a]1 Kin 8:45, 49; Ps 9:4; 18:27; 82:3
[b]Ps 12:5; 35:10

**Psalm 140:13**
[a]Ps 97:12
[b]Ps 11:7; 16:11; 17:15

## Targum

**Psa. 140:1** For praise; a psalm composed by David. ² Deliver me, O LORD, from an evil son of man; protect me from the man of rapacity. ³ Who have plotted evil things in the heart; all the day they incite wars. ⁴ They teach with their tongue like a snake; the venom of the spider is under their lips forever. ⁵ Protect me, O LORD, from the hand of wicked men; protect me from the man of rapacity; who have plotted to attack my steps. ⁶ The proud have hidden a trap for me, and they spread out ropes as a net beside the path; they have placed snares for me always. ⁷ I said to the LORD, "You are my God." Hear, O LORD, the sound of my petition. ⁸ God, the LORD, is the strength of my redemption; you have covered my head in the day of battle. ⁹ Do not grant, O LORD, the desires of Doeg the wicked; do not support his thoughts; let them be removed forever. ¹⁰ Ahithophel, head of the Sanhedrin of disciples — may the toil of the slander of their lips cover them. ¹¹ May coals from heaven come upon them; may he make them fall into the fire of Gehenna, in sparks that glow, lest they rise to eternal life. ¹² The man who speaks with deceitful tongue – they cannot dwell in the land of life; the angel of death will hunt down the men of evil rapacity, he will smite them in Gehenna. ¹³ Then it is manifest before me; for the LORD will work justice for the poor, justice for the needy. ¹⁴ Truly, the righteous will give thanks to your name; the upright will sit to pray before you.

## Spiritual Awareness

### Introduction

This Psalm reflects King David's dark and lonely feelings when Saul was chasing him. David knew that he was anointed to become Israel's king and that the LORD rejected Saul and his sons. David knew that the people chasing him were rejecting the LORD's decision to change Israel's leadership. The psalm also reflects that the Messiah would be a descendant of the House of David and divinely selected. The Messiah's task will be to gather the scattered Jews together and to fight the battle against Mog and Magog during the Messianic age.

### Superscript

**To the Sefirah Netzach who grants victory**

### Verse four

**They have sharpened their tongue like a serpent; viper's venom is beneath their lips. Meditate on this verse.**

### Verse six

**Who have proudly hidden snare and cords for me, who have spread a net for me by the wayside; they have a noose for me. Meditate on this verse.**

Verse nine

**Fulfill not, O LORD, the desires of the lawless, let me his aspiration grow so real that they could exalt themselves. Meditate on this verse.**

Notes on this Psalm

The last verse is the key to the Psalm. Only the righteous will render homage to the Name of the LORD. The people who follow the Laws of the LORD as defined in the Torah will be called righteous and their reward will be eternity in the LORD's house, the Lower Waters of Heaven.

# Psalm 141

| New American Standard 1995 | Hebrew |
| --- | --- |

**Psa. 141:0**   A Psalm of David.

**Psa. 141:1**   O LORD, I call upon You;
*a*hasten to me!

    *b*Give ear to my voice when I call
to You!
2    May my prayer be ¹counted as
*a*incense before You;

    The *b*lifting up of my hands as the
*c*evening offering.
3    Set a *a*guard, O LORD, ¹over my
mouth;

    Keep watch over the *b*door of my
lips.
4    *a*Do not incline my heart to any evil
thing,

    To practice deeds ¹of wickedness
With men who *b*do iniquity;
And *c*do not let me eat of their
delicacies.

**Psa. 141:5**   Let the *a*righteous smite me
¹in kindness and reprove me;

    It is *b*oil upon the head;
Do not let my head refuse it,
²For still my prayer *c*is ³against their
wicked deeds.
6    Their judges are *a*thrown down by
the sides of the rock,

    And they hear my words, for they
are pleasant.
7    As when one *a*plows and breaks
open the earth,

    Our *b*bones have been scattered at
the *c*mouth of ¹Sheol.

**Psa. 141:1** מִזְמֹ֗ור לְדָ֫וִ֥ד יְהוָ֣ה קְרָאתִ֑יךָ
ח֥וּשָׁה לִּ֑י הַאֲזִ֥ינָה קֹ֝ולִ֗י בְּקָרְאִי־לָֽךְ׃ ² תִּכֹּ֤ון
תְּפִלָּתִ֣י קְטֹ֣רֶת לְפָנֶ֑יךָ מַֽשְׂאַ֥ת כַּ֝פַּ֗י מִנְחַת־
עָֽרֶב׃ ³ שִׁיתָ֣ה יְ֭הוָה שָׁמְרָ֣ה לְפִ֑י נִ֝צְּרָ֗ה עַל־
דַּ֣ל שְׂפָתָֽי׃ ⁴ אַל־תַּט־לִבִּ֨י לְדָבָ֪ר ׀ רָ֡ע
לְהִתְעֹ֘ולֵ֤ל עֲלִלֹ֨ות ׀ בְּרֶ֗שַׁע אֶת־אִישִׁ֥ים
פֹּֽעֲלֵי־אָ֑וֶן וּבַל־אֶ֝לְחַ֗ם בְּמַנְעַמֵּיהֶֽם׃ ⁵
יֶֽהֶלְמֵֽנִי־צַדִּ֨יק ׀ חֶ֡סֶד וְֽיֹוכִיחֵ֗נִי שֶׁ֥מֶן רֹ֨אשׁ
אַל־יָנִ֪י רֹ֫אשִׁ֥י כִּי־עֹ֥וד וּתְפִלָּתִ֗י בְּרָעֹותֵיהֶֽם׃
⁶ נִשְׁמְט֣וּ בִֽידֵי־סֶ֭לַע שֹׁפְטֵיהֶ֑ם וְשָׁמְע֥וּ אֲ֝מָרַ֗י
כִּ֣י נָעֵֽמוּ׃ ⁷ כְּמֹ֤ו פֹלֵ֣חַ וּבֹקֵ֣עַ בָּאָ֑רֶץ נִפְזְר֥וּ
עֲ֝צָמֵ֗ינוּ לְפִ֣י שְׁאֹֽול׃ ⁸ כִּ֤י אֵלֶ֨יךָ ׀ יְהוִ֣ה אֲדֹנָ֣י
עֵינָ֑י בְּכָ֥ה חָ֝סִ֗יתִי אַל־תְּעַ֥ר נַפְשִֽׁי׃ ⁹ שָׁמְרֵ֗נִי
מִ֣ידֵי פַ֭ח יָ֣קְשׁוּ לִ֑י וּ֝מֹקְשֹׁ֗ות פֹּ֣עֲלֵי אָֽוֶן׃ ¹⁰
יִפְּל֣וּ בְמַכְמֹרָ֣יו רְשָׁעִ֑ים יַ֥חַד אָ֝נֹכִ֗י עַד־
אֶעֱבֹֽור׃

**Psa. 141:8**   For my *a*eyes are toward You, O [1]GOD, the Lord;

In You I *b*take refuge; *c*do not [2]leave me defenseless.

9   Keep me from the [1]*a*jaws of the trap which they have set for me,

And from the *b*snares of those who do iniquity.

10   Let the wicked *a*fall into their own nets,

While I pass by [1]*b*safely.

# References

**Psalm 141:1**
[a]Ps 22:19; 38:22; 70:5
[b]Ps 5:1; 143:1

**Psalm 141:2**
[1]Lit *fixed*
[a]Ex 30:8; Luke 1:10; Rev 5:8; 8:3, 4
[b]1 Tim 2:8
[c]Ex 29:39, 41; 1 Kin 18:29, 36; Dan 9:21

**Psalm 141:3**
[1]Lit *to*
[a]Ps 34:13; 39:1; Prov 13:3; 21:23
[b]Mic 7:5

**Psalm 141:4**
[1]Lit *in*
[a]Ps 119:36
[b]Is 32:6; Hos 6:8; Mal 3:15
[c]Prov 23:6

**Psalm 141:5**
[1]Or *lovingly*
[2]Lit *And my prayer*
[3]Or *in spite of their calamities*
[a]Prov 9:8; 19:25; 25:12; 27:6; Eccl 7:5; Gal 6:1
[b]Ps 23:5; 133:2
[c]Ps 35:14

**Psalm 141:6**
[a]2 Chr 25:12

**Psalm 141:7**
[1]I.e. the nether world
[a]Ps 129:3
[b]Ps 53:5
[c]Num 16:32, 33; Ps 88:3-5

**Psalm 141:8**
[1]Heb *YHWH,* usually rendered *LORD*

[2]Lit *pour out my soul*
[a]Ps 25:15; 123:2
[b]Ps 2:12; 11:1
[c]Ps 27:9

## Psalm 141:9

[1]Lit *hands of the trap*
[a]Ps 38:12; 64:5; 91:3; 119:110
[b]Ps 140:5

## Psalm 141:10

[1]Lit *altogether*
[a]Ps 7:15; 35:8; 57:6
[b]Ps 124:7

## Targum

**Psa. 141:1** A psalm of David. O LORD, I have called you; be concerned for me, hear my voice when I call to you. ² Let my prayer be directed before you like incense of spices, the upraising of my hands in prayer like a fragrant gift offered at evening. ³ Place, O LORD, a guard on my mouth, a keeper on the portal of my lips. ⁴ Do not incline my heart to anything evil, to think thoughts in wickedness to join with men who practice deceit, and I will not dine at the revels of their banquets. ⁵ The righteous man will strike me because of kindness, and rebuke me; the oil of holy anointing will not cease from my head, for still my prayer is marshaled against their evil. ⁶ They have withdrawn from the academy because of their harsh judgments; they turn and hear my words, for they are pleasant. ⁷ For like a man who labors and cleaves when plowing the earth, so are our limbs scattered on the mouth of the grave. ⁸ Therefore, unto you, God, the LORD, do my eyes look; I have hoped in your word, do not empty out my soul. ⁹ Protect me from the power of the trap they have hidden for me, and the snares of those who practice deceit. ¹⁰ May the wicked men fall into his nets together, until the time that I pass by.

## Spiritual Awareness

Introduction

King David composed this Psalm as he fled from Saul. David knew that Saul's anger was created by slanders people offered about David. He pleaded to the LORD for protection from the people chasing him and slandering him.

Notes on this Psalm

When something goes wrong in your life do you turn to the LORD for help? David certainly did all his life. Sometimes just talking to the LORD about your situation will help you solve it. The solution may come to you subconsciously. The Shekinah is with every person. Therefore, the Shekinah can influence a person to turn left or right. Never underestimate the power of the LORD through the Shekinah.

# Psalm 142

| New American Standard 1995 | Hebrew |
| --- | --- |
| **Psa. 142:0** [†]Maskil of David, when he was °in the cave. A Prayer.<br><br>**Psa. 142:1** I [a]cry aloud with my voice to the LORD;<br>I [b]make supplication with my voice to the LORD.<br>2 I [a]pour out my complaint before Him;<br>I declare my [b]trouble before Him.<br>3 When [a]my spirit [1]was overwhelmed within me,<br>You knew my path.<br>In the way where I walk<br>They have [b]hidden a trap for me.<br>4 Look to the right and see;<br>For there is [a]no one who regards me;<br>[1]There is no [b]escape for me;<br>[c]No one cares for my soul.<br><br>**Psa. 142:5** I cried out to You, O LORD;<br>I said, "You are [a]my refuge,<br>My [b]portion in the [c]land of the living.<br>6 "[a]Give heed to my cry,<br>For I am [b]brought very low;<br>Deliver me from my persecutors,<br>For they are too [c]strong for me.<br>7 "[a]Bring my soul out of prison,<br>So that I may give thanks to Your name;<br>The righteous will surround me, | **Psa. 142:1** מַשְׂכִּיל לְדָוִד בִּהְיוֹתוֹ בַמְּעָרָה תְפִלָּה: [2] קוֹלִי אֶל־יְהוָה אֶזְעָק קוֹלִי אֶל־יְהוָה אֶתְחַנָּן: [3] אֶשְׁפֹּךְ לְפָנָיו שִׂיחִי צָרָתִי לְפָנָיו אַגִּיד: [4] בְּהִתְעַטֵּף עָלַי רוּחִי וְאַתָּה יָדַעְתָּ נְתִיבָתִי בְּאֹרַח־זוּ אֲהַלֵּךְ טָמְנוּ פַח לִי: [5] הַבֵּיט יָמִין וּרְאֵה וְאֵין־לִי מַכִּיר אָבַד מָנוֹס מִמֶּנִּי אֵין דּוֹרֵשׁ לְנַפְשִׁי: [6] זָעַקְתִּי אֵלֶיךָ יְהוָה אָמַרְתִּי אַתָּה מַחְסִי חֶלְקִי בְּאֶרֶץ הַחַיִּים: [7] הַקְשִׁיבָה אֶל־רִנָּתִי כִּי־דַלּוֹתִי מְאֹד הַצִּילֵנִי מֵרֹדְפַי כִּי אָמְצוּ מִמֶּנִּי: [8] הוֹצִיאָה מִמַּסְגֵּר נַפְשִׁי לְהוֹדוֹת אֶת־שְׁמֶךָ בִּי יַכְתִּרוּ צַדִּיקִים כִּי תִגְמֹל עָלָי: |

| For You will [b]deal bountifully with me." | |
|---|---|

# References

**Psalm 142:0**
†Possibly *Contemplative,* or *Didactic,* or *Skillful Psalm*
°1 Sam 22:1; 24:3

**Psalm 142:1**
ᵃPs 77:1
ᵇPs 30:8

**Psalm 142:2**
ᵃPs 102: title
ᵇPs 77:2

**Psalm 142:3**
¹Lit *fainted*
ᵃPs 77:3; 143:4
ᵇPs 140:5

**Psalm 142:4**
¹Lit *Escape has perished from me*
ᵃPs 31:11; 88:8, 18
ᵇJob 11:20; Jer 25:35
ᶜJer 30:17

**Psalm 142:5**
ᵃPs 91:2, 9
ᵇPs 16:5; 73:26
ᶜPs 27:13

**Psalm 142:6**
ᵃPs 17:1
ᵇPs 79:8; 116:6
ᶜPs 18:17

**Psalm 142:7**
ᵃPs 143:11; 146:7
ᵇPs 13:6

## Targum

**Psa. 142:1** A good lesson, composed by David when he was in the cave; a prayer. [2] With my voice I will cry out in the presence of the LORD; with my voice I will pray in the presence of the LORD. [3] I will pour out my speech in his presence; I will tell of my trouble in his presence. [4] When my spirit grows weary against me, you know my path; on this road that I will walk, they have hidden a trap for me. [5] I looked to the right and saw, and there was no-one acknowledging me; deliverance has vanished from me, and there is none who avenges my soul. [6] I cried out to you, O LORD; I said, "You are my deliverer, my portion in the land of the living." [7] Hear my prayer, for I have become very poor; deliver me from my persecutors, for they are too strong for me. [8] Deliver my soul from prison, to confess your name; for my sake the righteous will make for you a glorious crown, for you will repay me with goodness.

## Spiritual Awareness

Introduction

David had a difficult time as he fled from Saul. The events of David's life emulated what Israel would go through centuries later. David was one person standing before a small army. Judah became a small nation with enemies that surrounded her. She needs to learn the lesson of how David survived. David called upon the LORD constantly to help him.

Notes on this Psalm

There are several Psalms which teach us to call upon the LORD for help during good and bad times. In this Psalm, David calls out to the LORD for help. When everything looks gloomy, call out to the LORD. Perhaps a better thing to do is to always pray to the LORD for help. Then if sometime terrible happens, the LORD will know your name and will come to your rescue.

# Psalm 143

| New American Standard 1995 | Hebrew |
| --- | --- |

**Psa. 143:1**    Hear my prayer, O LORD,

*a*Give ear to my supplications!

Answer me in Your *b*faithfulness,
in Your *c*righteousness!

2    And *a*do not enter into judgment
with Your servant,

For in Your sight *b*no man living is
righteous.

3    For the enemy has persecuted my
soul;

He has crushed my life *a*to the
ground;

He *b*has made me dwell in dark
places, like those who have long been
dead.

4    Therefore    *a*my    spirit    *1*is
overwhelmed within me;

My heart is *2b*appalled within me.

**Psa. 143:5**    I *a*remember the days of old;

I *b*meditate on all Your doings;

I *c*muse on the work of Your
hands.

6    I *a*stretch out my hands to You;

My *b*soul *longs* for You, as a
*1*parched land.    *2*Selah.

**Psa. 143:7**    *a*Answer me quickly, O
LORD, my *b*spirit fails;

*c*Do not hide Your face from me,

Or I will become like *d*those who
go down to the pit.

8    Let me hear Your *a*lovingkindness
*b*in the morning;

For I trust *c*in You;

מִזְמוֹר לְדָוִד יְהוָה ׀ שְׁמַ֖ע **Psa. 143:1**
תְפִלָּתִי הַאֲזִינָה אֶל־תַּחֲנוּנַי בֶּאֱמֻנָתְךָ עֲנֵ֖נִי
בְּצִדְקָתֶךָ ׃ 2 וְאַל־תָּבוֹא בְמִשְׁפָּט אֶת־עַבְדֶּךָ
כִּי לֹא־יִצְדַּק לְפָנֶיךָ כָל־חָ֖י ׃ 3 כִּי רָדַף אוֹיֵב
נַפְשִׁי דִּכָּא לָאָרֶץ חַיָּתִי הוֹשִׁיבַנִי בְמַחֲשַׁכִּים
כְּמֵתֵי עוֹלָם ׃ 4 וַתִּתְעַטֵּף עָלַי רוּחִי בְּתוֹכִי
יִשְׁתּוֹמֵם לִבִּי ׃ 5 זָכַרְתִּי יָמִים ׀ מִקֶּדֶם הָגִיתִי
בְכָל־פָּעֳלֶךָ בְּמַעֲשֵׂה יָדֶיךָ אֲשׂוֹחֵחַ ׃ 6
פֵּרַשְׂתִּי יָדַי אֵלֶיךָ נַפְשִׁי ׀ כְּאֶרֶץ־עֲיֵפָה לְךָ
סֶלָה ׃ 7 מַהֵר עֲנֵנִי ׀ יְהוָה כָּלְתָה רוּחִי אַל־
תַּסְתֵּר פָּנֶיךָ מִמֶּנִּי וְנִמְשַׁלְתִּי עִם־יֹרְדֵי בוֹר ׃ 8
הַשְׁמִיעֵנִי בַבֹּקֶר ׀ חַסְדֶּךָ כִּי־בְךָ בָטָחְתִּי
הוֹדִיעֵנִי דֶּרֶךְ־זוּ אֵלֵךְ כִּי־אֵלֶיךָ נָשָׂאתִי
נַפְשִׁי ׃ 9 הַצִּילֵנִי מֵאֹיְבַי ׀ יְהוָה אֵלֶיךָ כִסִּתִי ׃
10 לַמְּדֵנִי ׀ לַעֲשׂוֹת רְצוֹנֶךָ כִּי־אַתָּה אֱלוֹהָי
רוּחֲךָ טוֹבָה תַּנְחֵנִי בְּאֶרֶץ מִישׁוֹר ׃ 11 לְמַעַן־
שִׁמְךָ יְהוָה תְּחַיֵּנִי בְּצִדְקָתְךָ ׀ תוֹצִיא מִצָּרָה
נַפְשִׁי ׃ 12 וּבְחַסְדְּךָ תַּצְמִית אֹיְבָי וְהַאֲבַדְתָּ
כָּל־צֹרְרֵי נַפְשִׁי כִּי אֲנִי עַבְדֶּךָ ׃

Teach me the [d]way in which I should walk;

For to You I [e]lift up my soul.

9 [a]Deliver me, O LORD, from my enemies;

[1]I take refuge in You.

**Psa. 143:10** [a]Teach me to do Your will,

For You are my God;

Let [b]Your good Spirit [c]lead me on level [1]ground.

11 [a]For the sake of Your name, O LORD, [b]revive me.

[c]In Your righteousness bring my soul out of trouble.

12 And in Your lovingkindness, [1a]cut off my enemies

And [b]destroy all those who afflict my soul,

For [c]I am Your servant.

# References

**Psalm 143:1**
[a]Ps 140:6
[b]Ps 89:1, 2
[c]Ps 71:2

**Psalm 143:2**
[a]Job 14:3; 22:4
[b]1 Kin 8:46; Job 4:17; 9:2; 25:4; Ps 130:3; Eccl 7:20; Rom 3:10, 20; Gal 2:16

**Psalm 143:3**
[a]Ps 44:25
[b]Ps 88:6; Lam 3:6

**Psalm 143:4**
[1]Lit *faints*
[2]Or *desolate*
[a]Ps 77:3; 142:3
[b]Lam 3:11

**Psalm 143:5**
[a]Ps 77:5, 10, 11
[b]Ps 77:12
[c]Ps 105:2

**Psalm 143:6**
[1]Lit *weary*
[2]*Selah* may mean: *Pause, Crescendo* or *Musical interlude*
[a]Job 11:13; Ps 88:9
[b]Ps 42:2; 63:1

**Psalm 143:7**
[a]Ps 69:17
[b]Ps 73:26; 84:2; Jer 8:18; Lam 1:22
[c]Ps 27:9; 69:17; 102:2
[d]Ps 28:1; 88:4

**Psalm 143:8**
[a]Ps 90:14

[b]Ps 46:5
[c]Ps 25:2
[d]Ps 27:11; 32:8; 86:11
[e]Ps 25:1; 86:4

**Psalm 143:9**
[1]Lit *To You have I hidden*
[a]Ps 31:15; 59:1

**Psalm 143:10**
[1]Lit *land*
[a]Ps 25:4, 5; 119:12
[b]Neh 9:20
[c]Ps 23:3

**Psalm 143:11**
[a]Ps 25:11
[b]Ps 119:25
[c]Ps 31:1; 71:2

**Psalm 143:12**
[1]Or *silence*
[a]Ps 54:5
[b]Ps 52:5
[c]Ps 116:16

## Targum

**Psa. 143:1** A praise for David. O LORD, hear my prayer, listen to my supplication; in your truth answer me, in your generosity. **2** And do not enter the house of judgment with your servant, for nothing that lives will be pure in your presence. **3** For the enemy is persecuting my soul; he has crushed my life to the earth; he made me dwell in darkness like those who are dead in this age. **4** When my soul grows weary against me, in my body my heart will be confounded. **5** I called to mind the days of old; I meditated on all your deeds; I will speak of the works of your hands. **6** I spread out my hands in prayer before you; my soul looks towards you forever like a land that is thirsty for water. **7** Hurry, answer me, O LORD; my spirit yearned for you; do not remove your presence from me; and I have become like those who descend to the pit of the grave. **8** Proclaim your goodness to me in the morning, for I have hoped in your word; make me know this way that I walk, for to you have I lifted up my soul in prayer. **9** Deliver me from my enemies, O LORD; I have reckoned your word to be redeeming. **10** Teach me to do your will, for you are my God; your good holy spirit will guide me in the land correctly. **11** For the sake of your name, O LORD, sustain me; by your righteousness bring my soul out of distress. **12** And by your kindness overthrow my enemies, and destroy all those who oppress my soul, for I am your servant. --

## Spiritual Awareness

Introduction

This Psalm is a continuation of Psalm 142.


Notes on this Psalm

Throughout the Psalm David calls upon the Sefirah Chesed for the LORD's lovingkindness.

## Psalm 144

| New American Standard 1995 | Hebrew |
|---|---|

**Psa. 144:0**   *A Psalm* of David.

**Psa. 144:1**   Blessed be the LORD, *a*my rock,

Who *b*trains my hands for war,
*And* my fingers for battle;
2   My lovingkindness and *a*my fortress,

My *b*stronghold and my deliverer,
My *c*shield and He in whom I take refuge,

Who *d*subdues ¹my people under me.
3   O LORD, *a*what is man, that You take knowledge of him?

Or the son of man, that You think of him?
4   *a*Man is like a mere breath;
His *b*days are like a passing shadow.

**Psa. 144:5**   *a*Bow Your heavens, O LORD, and *b*come down;

*c*Touch the mountains, that they may smoke.
6   Flash forth *a*lightning and scatter them;

Send out Your *b*arrows and confuse them.
7   Stretch forth Your hand *a*from on high;

Rescue me and *b*deliver me out of great waters,

Out of the hand of *c*aliens
8   Whose mouths *a*speak deceit,
And whose *b*right hand is a right hand of falsehood.

לְדָוִד ׀ בָּרוּךְ יְהוָה ׀ צוּרִי **Psa. 144:1**
הַמְלַמֵּד יָדַי לַקְרָב אֶצְבְּעוֹתַי לַמִּלְחָמָה ׃ 2
חַסְדִּי וּמְצוּדָתִי מִשְׂגַּבִּי וּמְפַלְטִי לִי מָגִנִּי וּבוֹ
חָסִיתִי הָרוֹדֵד עַמִּי תַחְתָּי ׃ 3 יְהוָה מָה־אָדָם
וַתֵּדָעֵהוּ בֶּן־אֱנוֹשׁ וַתְּחַשְּׁבֵהוּ ׃ 4 אָדָם לַהֶבֶל
דָּמָה יָמָיו כְּצֵל עוֹבֵר ׃ 5 יְהוָה הַט־שָׁמֶיךָ
וְתֵרֵד גַּע בֶּהָרִים וְיֶעֱשָׁנוּ ׃ 6 בְּרוֹק בָּרָק
וּתְפִיצֵם שְׁלַח חִצֶּיךָ וּתְהֻמֵּם ׃ 7 שְׁלַח יָדֶיךָ
מִמָּרוֹם פְּצֵנִי וְהַצִּילֵנִי מִמַּיִם רַבִּים מִיַּד בְּנֵי
נֵכָר ׃ 8 אֲשֶׁר פִּיהֶם דִּבֶּר־שָׁוְא וִימִינָם יְמִין
שָׁקֶר ׃ 9 אֱלֹהִים שִׁיר חָדָשׁ אָשִׁירָה לָּךְ בְּנֵבֶל
עָשׂוֹר אֲזַמְּרָה־לָּךְ ׃ 10 הַנּוֹתֵן תְּשׁוּעָה
לַמְּלָכִים הַפּוֹצֶה אֶת־דָּוִד עַבְדּוֹ מֵחֶרֶב
רָעָה ׃ 11 פְּצֵנִי וְהַצִּילֵנִי מִיַּד בְּנֵי־נֵכָר אֲשֶׁר
פִּיהֶם דִּבֶּר־שָׁוְא וִימִינָם יְמִין שָׁקֶר ׃ 12 אֲשֶׁר
בָּנֵינוּ ׀ כִּנְטִעִים מְגֻדָּלִים בִּנְעוּרֵיהֶם בְּנוֹתֵינוּ
כְזָוִיֹּת מְחֻטָּבוֹת תַּבְנִית הֵיכָל ׃ 13 מְזָוֵינוּ
מְלֵאִים מְפִיקִים מִזַּן אֶל־זַן צֹאונֵנוּ מַאֲלִיפוֹת
מְרֻבָּבוֹת בְּחוּצוֹתֵינוּ ׃ 14 אַלּוּפֵינוּ מְסֻבָּלִים
אֵין־פֶּרֶץ וְאֵין יוֹצֵאת וְאֵין צְוָחָה בִּרְחֹבֹתֵינוּ ׃
15 אַשְׁרֵי הָעָם שֶׁכָּכָה לּוֹ אַשְׁרֵי הָעָם שֶׁיֲהוָה
אֱלֹהָיו ׃

**Psa. 144:9**  I will sing a *a*new song to You, O God;

　　Upon a *b*harp of ten strings I will sing praises to You,

**10**　　Who *a*gives salvation to kings,

　　Who *b*rescues David His servant from the evil sword.

**11**　　Rescue me and deliver me out of the hand of *a*aliens,

　　Whose mouth *b*speaks deceit

　　And whose *c*right hand is a right hand of falsehood.

**Psa. 144:12**　　Let our sons in their youth be as *a*grown-up plants,

　　And our daughters as *b*corner pillars *1*fashioned as for a palace;

**13**　　Let our *a*garners be full, furnishing every kind of produce,

　　*And* our flocks bring forth thousands and ten thousands in our *1*fields;

**14**　　Let our *a*cattle *1*bear

　　Without *2b*mishap and without *3c*loss,

　　*Let there be* no *d*outcry in our streets!

**15**　　How blessed are the people who are so situated;

　　How *a*blessed are the people whose God is the LORD!

# References

**Psalm 144:1**
[a]Ps 18:2
[b]2 Sam 22:35; Ps 18:34

**Psalm 144:2**
[1]Another reading is *peoples*
[a]Ps 18:2; 91:2
[b]Ps 59:9
[c]Ps 3:3; 28:7; 84:9
[d]Ps 18:39

**Psalm 144:3**
[a]Job 7:17; Ps 8:4; Heb 2:6

**Psalm 144:4**
[a]Ps 39:11
[b]Job 8:9; 14:2; Ps 102:11; 109:23

**Psalm 144:5**
[a]Ps 18:9
[b]Is 64:1
[c]Ps 104:32

**Psalm 144:6**
[a]Ps 18:14
[b]Ps 7:13; 58:7; Hab 3:11; Zech 9:14

**Psalm 144:7**
[a]Ps 18:16
[b]Ps 69:1, 14
[c]Ps 18:44; 54:3

**Psalm 144:8**
[a]Ps 12:2; 41:6
[b]Gen 14:22; Deut 32:40; Ps 106:26; Is 44:20

**Psalm 144:9**
[a]Ps 33:3; 40:3

[b]Ps 33:2

**Psalm 144:10**
[a]Ps 18:50
[b]2 Sam 18:7; Ps 140:7

**Psalm 144:11**
[a]Ps 18:44; 54:3
[b]Ps 12:2; 41:6
[c]Gen 14:22; Deut 32:40; Ps 106:26; Is 44:20

**Psalm 144:12**
[1]Lit *cut after the pattern of*
[a]Ps 92:12-14; 128:3
[b]Song 4:4; 7:4

**Psalm 144:13**
[1]Lit *outside*
[a]Prov 3:9, 10

**Psalm 144:14**
[1]Lit *be laden*
[2]Lit *bursting forth*
[3]Lit *going out*
[a]Prov 14:4
[b]2 Kin 25:10, 11
[c]Amos 5:3
[d]Is 24:11; Jer 14:2

**Psalm 144:15**
[a]Ps 33:12

## Targum

**Psa. 144:1** Composed by David. Blessed is the LORD, my strength, who instructs my hands for battle, my fingers to wage war. **²** He who acts favorably, and my mighty fortress; my strength, and the one who delivers me; my shield, and I have hoped in his word; he who tramples the Gentiles under me. **³** O LORD, what is a son of man, that you know him? The sons of men, that you think of him? **⁴** A son of man is likened to nothing; his days are like a shadow that passes. **⁵** O LORD, bend the heavens and be revealed; touch the mountains, and they send up smoke. **⁶** Make lightning flash, and scatter them; send arrows and confound them. **⁷** Extend your hand from highest heaven; deliver me and save me from the hordes that are likened to many waters, from the hand of the sons of foreigners. **⁸** Whose mouth speaks vain oaths, and their Torah is a Torah of deceit. **⁹** God, I will sing a new psalm in your presence; with the lyre of ten strings I will make music in your presence. **¹⁰** Who gives redemption to kings, who delivers David his servant from the wicked sword of Goliath. **¹¹** Deliver me and save me from the hands of the sons of foreigners, whose mouth speaks vain oaths, and their Torah is a Torah of deceit. **¹²** For our sons are like plantings of date-palms, growing in the learning of Torah from their youth; our daughters are beautiful and fit for priests who serve within the temple. **¹³** Our treasuries are full, supplying needs from year to year; our flocks are bearing thousands, they increase by tens of thousands in our streets. **¹⁴** Our oxen bear great loads; there is no harshness and no expression of evil; there is no clamor of weeping in our squares. **¹⁵** Happy the people for whom it is thus; happy the people whose God is the LORD.

## Spiritual Awareness

### Introduction

This is a Psalm composed by David. It is a Psalm of thanksgiving and praise at the beginning of his reign after the LORD granted him victory over his enemies. In the Psalm, David expressed the Jewish attitude toward war and warriors. The triumphant soldier has no claim to success, for he is only a tool in the LORD's hands.

### Notes on this Psalm

Do you praise the LORD if things are going well in your life? Numerous times people take the LORD for granted until something terrible happens. Then they go to their place of worship and pled with the LORD for help. People must remember that the good things in their lives come from the LORD. The bad things are usually caused by freewill or the influence of Evil Inclination. Prayer should comprise praising the LORD for the triumphant of life and for help when bad things happen.

# Psalm 145

| New American Standard 1995 | Hebrew |
| --- | --- |

**Psa. 145:0**  *A Psalm* of Praise, of David.

**Psa. 145:1**  I will *a*extol You, *b*my God, O King,

And I will *c*bless Your name forever and ever.

2  Every day I will bless You,

And I will *a*praise Your name forever and ever.

3  *a*Great is the LORD, and highly to be praised,

And His *b*greatness is unsearchable.

4  One *a*generation shall praise Your works to another,

And shall declare Your mighty acts.

5  On the *a*glorious ¹splendor of Your majesty

And *b*on Your wonderful works, I will meditate.

6  Men shall speak of the ¹power of Your *a*awesome acts,

And I will *b*tell of Your greatness.

7  They shall ¹eagerly utter the memory of Your *a*abundant goodness

And will *b*shout joyfully of Your righteousness.

**Psa. 145:8**  The LORD is *a*gracious and merciful;

Slow to anger and great in lovingkindness.

9  The LORD is *a*good to all,

תְּהִלָּה לְדָוִד אֲרוֹמִמְךָ אֱלוֹהַי **Psa. 145:1**
הַמֶּלֶךְ וַאֲבָרְכָה שִׁמְךָ לְעוֹלָם וָעֶד: ² בְּכָל־
יוֹם אֲבָרְכֶךָּ וַאֲהַלְלָה שִׁמְךָ לְעוֹלָם וָעֶד: ³
גָּדוֹל יְהוָה וּמְהֻלָּל מְאֹד וְלִגְדֻלָּתוֹ אֵין חֵקֶר:
⁴ דּוֹר לְדוֹר יְשַׁבַּח מַעֲשֶׂיךָ וּגְבוּרֹתֶיךָ יַגִּידוּ:
⁵ הֲדַר כְּבוֹד הוֹדֶךָ וְדִבְרֵי נִפְלְאֹתֶיךָ
אָשִׂיחָה: ⁶ וֶעֱזוּז נוֹרְאֹתֶיךָ יֹאמֵרוּ וּגְדוּלָּתֶיךָ
[וּ]גְדוּלָתְךָ] אֲסַפְּרֶנָּה: ⁷ זֵכֶר רַב־טוּבְךָ
יַבִּיעוּ וְצִדְקָתְךָ יְרַנֵּנוּ: ⁸ חַנּוּן וְרַחוּם יְהוָה
אֶרֶךְ אַפַּיִם וּגְדָל־חָסֶד: ⁹ טוֹב־יְהוָה לַכֹּל
וְרַחֲמָיו עַל־כָּל־מַעֲשָׂיו: ¹⁰ יוֹדוּךָ יְהוָה כָּל־
מַעֲשֶׂיךָ וַחֲסִידֶיךָ יְבָרְכוּכָה: ¹¹ כְּבוֹד
מַלְכוּתְךָ יֹאמֵרוּ וּגְבוּרָתְךָ יְדַבֵּרוּ: ¹²
לְהוֹדִיעַ ׀ לִבְנֵי הָאָדָם גְּבוּרֹתָיו וּכְבוֹד הֲדַר
מַלְכוּתוֹ: ¹³ מַלְכוּתְךָ מַלְכוּת כָּל־עֹלָמִים
וּמֶמְשַׁלְתְּךָ בְּכָל־דּוֹר וָדוֹר: ¹⁴ סוֹמֵךְ יְהוָה
לְכָל־הַנֹּפְלִים וְזוֹקֵף לְכָל־הַכְּפוּפִים: ¹⁵
עֵינֵי־כֹל אֵלֶיךָ יְשַׂבֵּרוּ וְאַתָּה נוֹתֵן־לָהֶם אֶת־
אָכְלָם בְּעִתּוֹ: ¹⁶ פּוֹתֵחַ אֶת־יָדֶךָ וּמַשְׂבִּיעַ
לְכָל־חַי רָצוֹן: ¹⁷ צַדִּיק יְהוָה בְּכָל־דְּרָכָיו
וְחָסִיד בְּכָל־מַעֲשָׂיו: ¹⁸ קָרוֹב יְהוָה לְכָל־
קֹרְאָיו לְכֹל אֲשֶׁר יִקְרָאֻהוּ בֶאֱמֶת: ¹⁹ רְצוֹן
יְרֵאָיו יַעֲשֶׂה וְאֶת־שַׁוְעָתָם יִשְׁמַע וְיוֹשִׁיעֵם: ²⁰
שׁוֹמֵר יְהוָה אֶת־כָּל־אֹהֲבָיו וְאֵת כָּל־
הָרְשָׁעִים יַשְׁמִיד: ²¹ תְּהִלַּת יְהוָה יְדַבֶּר־פִּי
וִיבָרֵךְ כָּל־בָּשָׂר שֵׁם קָדְשׁוֹ לְעוֹלָם וָעֶד:

And His [b]mercies are over all His works.

**10** [a]All Your works shall give thanks to You, O LORD,

And Your [b]godly ones shall bless You.

**11** They shall speak of the [a]glory of Your kingdom

And talk of Your power;

**12** To [a]make known to the sons of men [1]Your mighty acts

And the [b]glory of the majesty of [1]Your kingdom.

**13** Your kingdom is [1]an [a]everlasting kingdom,

And Your dominion *endures* throughout all generations.

**Psa. 145:14** The LORD [a]sustains all who fall

And [b]raises up all who are bowed down.

**15** The eyes of all [1]look to You,

And You [a]give them their food in due time.

**16** You [a]open Your hand

And satisfy the desire of every living thing.

**Psa. 145:17** The LORD is [a]righteous in all His ways

And kind in all His deeds.

**18** The LORD is [a]near to all who call upon Him,

To all who call upon Him [b]in truth.

**19** He will [a]fulfill the desire of those who fear Him;

He will also [b]hear their cry and will save them.

**20** The LORD [a]keeps all who love Him,

|  |  |
|---|---|
| But all the [b]wicked He will destroy.<br>21  My [a]mouth will speak the praise of the LORD,<br>And [b]all flesh will [c]bless His holy name forever and ever. |  |

# References

**Psalm 145:1**
[a]Ps 30:1; 66:17
[b]Ps 5:2
[c]Ps 34:1

**Psalm 145:2**
[a]Ps 71:6

**Psalm 145:3**
[a]Ps 48:1; 86:10; 147:5
[b]Job 5:9; 9:10; 11:7; Is 40:28; Rom 11:33

**Psalm 145:4**
[a]Ps 22:30, 31; Is 38:19

**Psalm 145:5**
[1]Or *majesty of Your splendor*
[a]Ps 145:12
[b]Ps 119:27

**Psalm 145:6**
[1]Or *strength*
[a]Deut 10:21; Ps 66:3; 106:22
[b]Deut 32:3

**Psalm 145:7**
[1]Or *bubble over with*
[a]Ps 31:19; Is 63:7
[b]Ps 51:14

**Psalm 145:8**
[a]Ex 34:6; Num 14:18; Ps 86:5, 15; 103:8

**Psalm 145:9**
[a]Ps 100:5; 136:1; Jer 33:11; Nah 1:7; Matt 19:17; Mark 10:18
[b]Ps 145:15

**Psalm 145:10**

[a]Ps 19:1; 103:22
[b]Ps 68:26

**Psalm 145:11**
[a]Jer 14:21

**Psalm 145:12**
[1]Lit *His*
[a]Ps 105:1
[b]Ps 145:5; Is 2:10, 19, 21

**Psalm 145:13**
[1]Lit *a kingdom of all ages*
[a]Ps 10:16; 29:10; 1 Tim 1:17; 2 Pet 1:11

**Psalm 145:14**
[a]Ps 37:24
[b]Ps 146:8

**Psalm 145:15**
[1]Lit *wait;* or *hope for*
[a]Ps 104:27; 136:25

**Psalm 145:16**
[a]Ps 104:28

**Psalm 145:17**
[a]Ps 116:5

**Psalm 145:18**
[a]Deut 4:7; Ps 34:18; 119:151
[b]John 4:24

**Psalm 145:19**
[a]Ps 21:2; 37:4
[b]Ps 10:17; Prov 15:29; 1 John 5:14

**Psalm 145:20**
[a]Ps 31:23; 91:14; 97:10
[b]Ps 9:5; 37:38

**Psalm 145:21**
[a]Ps 71:8
[b]Ps 65:2; 150:6
[c]Ps 145:1, 2

## Targum

**Psa. 145:1** A psalm of David. I will exalt you, O my God the king, and I will bless your name for ages upon ages. [2] Every day I will bless you and I will praise your name for ages upon ages. [3] Great is the LORD and very praiseworthy; and there is no end to his greatness. [4] Each generation will praise your work to the next, and they will tell of your wonders. [5] The splendor of the glory of your majesty, and the words of your wonders, I will speak. [6] And they will utter the strength of your fear, and they will tell of your greatness. [7] They will spread abroad the memory of your abundant goodness, and they will praise your generosity. [8] Compassionate and merciful is the LORD, putting away anger and doing many good things. [9] The LORD is good to all, and his mercies are over all his works. [10] All your works shall give you thanks, O LORD, and your pious ones shall bless you. [11] They will utter the glory of your kingdom, and will speak of your might. [12] To make known his powerful deeds to the sons of men, and the glorious splendor of his kingdom. [13] Your kingdom is a kingdom of all ages, and your dominion is in every generation. [14] The LORD supports all who have fallen, and lifts up all who are bowed down. [15] The eyes of all look hopefully to you, and you give them their food in its season. [16] You open your hand, and satisfy the desire of every living thing. [17] The LORD is just in all his ways, and gracious in all his works. [18] The LORD is near to all who call on him, to all who call on him in truth. [19] He will do the will of those who fear him, and he will hear their petition and redeem them. [20] The LORD protects all who love him, but he will destroy all the wicked. [21] My mouth will speak the praise of the LORD, and all the sons of flesh will bless his holy name for ages upon ages.

## Spiritual Awareness

Introduction

This Psalm is arranged with the first word of each verse are the initial letter of the alphabet in alphabetical order. This work is fundamental, as basic as the alphabet. The Psalm also emphasizes the LORD's most crucial function is to supply the physical needs of all creation.

Notes on this Psalm

Humans are stewards of the LORD's creation. Since material items from Earth cannot be taken, in to the Lower Waters of Heaven the person owning the item is a steward. The gold that David had as King is somewhere today. The same thing applies to everything material. That is why it is important to develop spirituality. This is the one thing that your soul can take from Earth into the Lower Waters. It is an essential part of the reason humanity is here on earth. Too many people ignore their spirituality. This mainly comprises knowing about the LORD, learning the ways of the LORD, and offering praise to the LORD.

# Psalm 146

| New American Standard 1995 | Hebrew |
| --- | --- |

**Psa. 146:1**    [1]Praise [2]the LORD!

[a]Praise the LORD, O my soul!

[2]    I will praise the LORD [a]while I live;

I will [b]sing praises to my God while I have my being.

[3]    [a]Do not trust in princes,

In [1]mortal [b]man, in whom there is [c]no salvation.

[4]    His [a]spirit departs, he [b]returns to [1]the earth;

In that very day his [c]thoughts perish.

[5]    How [a]blessed is he whose help is the God of Jacob,

Whose [b]hope is in the LORD his God,

[6]    Who [a]made heaven and earth,

The [b]sea and all that is in them;

Who [c]keeps [1]faith forever;

[7]    Who [a]executes justice for the oppressed;

Who [b]gives food to the hungry.

The LORD [c]sets the prisoners free.

**Psa. 146:8**    The LORD [a]opens *the eyes of* the blind;

The LORD [b]raises up those who are bowed down;

The LORD [c]loves the righteous;

[9]    The LORD [1a]protects the [2]strangers;

He [3b]supports the fatherless and the widow,

הַלְלוּ־יָהּ הַלְלִי נַפְשִׁי אֶת־יְהוָה: **Psa. 146:1**
[2] אֲהַלְלָה יְהוָה בְּחַיָּי אֲזַמְּרָה לֵאלֹהַי
בְּעוֹדִי: [3] אַל־תִּבְטְחוּ בִנְדִיבִים בְּבֶן־אָדָם ׀
שֶׁאֵין לוֹ תְשׁוּעָה: [4] תֵּצֵא רוּחוֹ יָשֻׁב לְאַדְמָתוֹ
בַּיּוֹם הַהוּא אָבְדוּ עֶשְׁתֹּנֹתָיו: [5] אַשְׁרֵי שֶׁאֵל
יַעֲקֹב בְּעֶזְרוֹ שִׂבְרוֹ עַל־יְהוָה אֱלֹהָיו: [6] עֹשֶׂה
׀ שָׁמַיִם וָאָרֶץ אֶת־הַיָּם וְאֶת־כָּל־אֲשֶׁר־בָּם
הַשֹּׁמֵר אֱמֶת לְעוֹלָם: [7] עֹשֶׂה מִשְׁפָּט ׀
לָעֲשׁוּקִים נֹתֵן לֶחֶם לָרְעֵבִים יְהוָה מַתִּיר
אֲסוּרִים: [8] יְהוָה ׀ פֹּקֵחַ עִוְרִים יְהוָה זֹקֵף
כְּפוּפִים יְהוָה אֹהֵב צַדִּיקִים: [9] יְהוָה ׀ שֹׁמֵר
אֶת־גֵּרִים יָתוֹם וְאַלְמָנָה יְעוֹדֵד וְדֶרֶךְ
רְשָׁעִים יְעַוֵּת: [10] יִמְלֹךְ יְהוָה ׀ לְעוֹלָם
אֱלֹהַיִךְ צִיּוֹן לְדֹר וָדֹר הַלְלוּ־יָהּ:

| | |
|---|---|
| But He [4]thwarts ʿthe way of the wicked. | |

# References

**Psalm 146:1**
[1]Or *Hallelujah!*
[2]Heb *YAH*
[a]Ps 103:1

**Psalm 146:2**
[a]Ps 63:4
[b]Ps 104:33

**Psalm 146:3**
[1]Lit *a son of a man*
[a]Ps 118:9
[b]Ps 118:8; Is 2:22
[c]Ps 60:11; 108:12

**Psalm 146:4**
[1]Lit *his earth*
[a]Ps 104:29
[b]Eccl 12:7
[c]Ps 33:10; 1 Cor 2:6

**Psalm 146:5**
[a]Ps 144:15; Jer 17:7
[b]Ps 71:5

**Psalm 146:6**
[1]Or *truth*
[a]Ps 115:15; Rev 14:7
[b]Acts 14:15
[c]Ps 117:2

**Psalm 146:7**
[a]Ps 103:6
[b]Ps 107:9; 145:15
[c]Ps 68:6; Is 61:1

**Psalm 146:8**
[a]Matt 9:30; John 9:7

[b]Ps 145:14
[c]Ps 11:7

**Psalm 146:9**
[1]Or *keeps*
[2]Or *sojourners*
[3]Or *relieves*
[4]Lit *makes crooked*
[a]Ex 22:21; Lev 19:34
[b]Deut 10:18; Ps 68:5
[c]Ps 147:6

**Psalm 146:10**
[1]Or *Hallelujah!*
[2]Heb *YAH*
[a]Ex 15:18; Ps 10:16

## Targum

**Psa. 146:1** Hallelujah! Praise the name of the LORD, O my soul. [2] I will sing praise, O LORD, in my lifetime, I will make music to my God while I exist. [3] You shall not place your trust in rulers, in a son of man who has no redemption. [4] His spirit will go away, he will return to his dust; on that day his plans perish. [5] Happy is he whose help is the God of Jacob, whose hope is in the LORD his God. [6] Who made heaven and earth, the sea and all that is in them, who keeps truth forever. [7] Who brings judgment for the oppressed, who gives food to the hungry; the LORD, who sets the prisoners free. [8] The LORD gives sight to foreigners, who are likened to the blind; the LORD lifts up those who are bowed down, the LORD loves the righteous. [9] The LORD protects the proselyte; he will support the widow and orphan, but will confound the way of the wicked. [10] The LORD will reign forever; your God, O Zion, for all generations. Hallelujah!

## Spiritual Awareness

Introduction

This is a Psalm of hope and encouragement for the oppressed Jews in Exile in Babylon. The torture of being in Exile was a concern. The author wants to help the people to continue to praise the LORD even in Exile.

Notes on this Psalm

The Psalmist notes that there are people who place their ultimate trust in men and women. One's ultimate trust should be in the LORD. It is fine to trust people, but the ultimate trust should only be in the LORD.

# Psalm 147

| New American Standard 1995 | Hebrew |
|---|---|

**Psa. 147:1**    [1]Praise [2]the LORD!
　　For [a]it is good to sing praises to
our God;
　　For [3]it is pleasant *and* praise is
[b]becoming.
2　　The LORD [a]builds up Jerusalem;
　　He [b]gathers the outcasts of Israel.
3　　He heals the [a]brokenhearted
　　And [b]binds up their [1]wounds.
4　　He [a]counts the number of the
stars;
　　He [1b]gives names to all of them.
5　　[a]Great is our Lord and abundant
in strength;
　　His [b]understanding is [1]infinite.
6　　The LORD [1a]supports the
afflicted;
　　He brings down the wicked to the
ground.

**Psa. 147:7**    [a]Sing to the LORD with
thanksgiving;
　　Sing praises to our God on the
lyre,
8　　Who [a]covers the heavens with
clouds,
　　Who [b]provides rain for the earth,
　　Who [c]makes grass to [1]grow on the
mountains.
9　　He [a]gives to the beast its food,
　　*And* to the [b]young ravens which
cry.
10　　He does not delight in the
strength of the [a]horse;

Psa. 147:1 הַלְלוּ יָהּ ׀ כִּי־טוֹב זַמְּרָה

2 אֱלֹהֵינוּ כִּי־נָעִים נָאוָה תְהִלָּה :

בּוֹנֵה יְרוּשָׁלִַם יְהוָה נִדְחֵי יִשְׂרָאֵל

3 יְכַנֵּס : הָרֹפֵא לִשְׁבוּרֵי לֵב

4 וּמְחַבֵּשׁ לְעַצְּבוֹתָם : מוֹנֶה מִסְפָּר

5 לַכּוֹכָבִים לְכֻלָּם שֵׁמוֹת יִקְרָא :

גָּדוֹל אֲדוֹנֵינוּ וְרַב־כֹּחַ לִתְבוּנָתוֹ

6 אֵין מִסְפָּר : מְעוֹדֵד עֲנָוִים יְהוָה

7 מַשְׁפִּיל רְשָׁעִים עֲדֵי־אָרֶץ : עֱנוּ

לַיהוָה בְּתוֹדָה זַמְּרוּ לֵאלֹהֵינוּ

8 בְכִנּוֹר : הַמְכַסֶּה שָׁמַיִם ׀ בְּעָבִים

הַמֵּכִין לָאָרֶץ מָטָר הַמַּצְמִיחַ הָרִים

9 חָצִיר : נוֹתֵן לִבְהֵמָה לַחְמָהּ לִבְנֵי

10 עֹרֵב אֲשֶׁר יִקְרָאוּ : לֹא בִגְבוּרַת

הַסּוּס יֶחְפָּץ לֹא־בְשׁוֹקֵי הָאִישׁ

11 יִרְצֶה : רוֹצֶה יְהוָה אֶת־יְרֵאָיו

12 אֶת־הַמְיַחֲלִים לְחַסְדּוֹ : שַׁבְּחִי

יְרוּשָׁלִַם אֶת־יְהוָה הַלְלִי אֱלֹהַיִךְ

13 צִיּוֹן : כִּי־חִזַּק בְּרִיחֵי שְׁעָרָיִךְ

14 בֵּרַךְ בָּנַיִךְ בְּקִרְבֵּךְ : הַשָּׂם־

גְּבוּלֵךְ שָׁלוֹם חֵלֶב חִטִּים יַשְׂבִּיעֵךְ :

15 הַשֹּׁלֵחַ אִמְרָתוֹ אָרֶץ עַד־מְהֵרָה

16 יָרוּץ דְּבָרוֹ : הַנֹּתֵן שֶׁלֶג כַּצָּמֶר

17 כְּפוֹר כָּאֵפֶר יְפַזֵּר : מַשְׁלִיךְ

He <sup>b</sup>does not take pleasure in the legs of a man.

11      The LORD <sup>a</sup>favors those who fear Him,

<sup>b</sup>Those who wait for His lovingkindness.

**Psa. 147:12**      Praise the LORD, O Jerusalem!

Praise your God, O Zion!

13      For He has strengthened the <sup>a</sup>bars of your gates;

He has <sup>b</sup>blessed your sons within you.

14      He <sup>a</sup>makes <sup>1</sup>peace in your borders;

He <sup>b</sup>satisfies you with <sup>c</sup>the <sup>2</sup>finest of the wheat.

15      He sends forth His <sup>a</sup>command to the earth;

His <sup>b</sup>word runs very swiftly.

16      He gives <sup>a</sup>snow like wool;

He scatters the <sup>b</sup>frost like ashes.

17      He casts forth His <sup>a</sup>ice as fragments;

Who can stand before His <sup>b</sup>cold?

18      He <sup>a</sup>sends forth His word and melts them;

He <sup>b</sup>causes His wind to blow and the waters to flow.

19      He <sup>a</sup>declares His words to Jacob,

His <sup>b</sup>statutes and His ordinances to Israel.

20      He <sup>a</sup>has not dealt thus with any nation;

And as for His ordinances, they have <sup>b</sup>not known them.

<sup>1</sup>Praise <sup>2</sup>the LORD!

קָֽרְחֹוֹ כְפִתֶּים לִפְנֵי קָרָתֹוֹ מִי
יַעֲמֹד ׃ 18 יִשְׁלַח דְּבָרֹו וְיַמְסֵם יַשֵּׁב
רוּחֹו יִזְּלוּ־מָיִם ׃ 19 מַגִּיד דְּבָרֹו
[דְּבָרָיו] לְיַעֲקֹב חֻקָּיו וּמִשְׁפָּטָיו
לְיִשְׂרָאֵל ׃ 20 לֹא עָשָׂה כֵן ׀ לְכָל־
גֹּוי וּמִשְׁפָּטִים בַּל־יְדָעֹוּם הַלְלוּ־
יָהּ ׃

# References

**Psalm 147:1**
[1]Or *Hallelujah!*
[2]Heb *YAH*
[3]Or *He is gracious*
[a]Ps 92:1; 135:3
[b]Ps 33:1

**Psalm 147:2**
[a]Ps 51:18; 102:16
[b]Deut 30:3; Ps 106:47; Is 11:12; 56:8; Ezek 39:28

**Psalm 147:3**
[1]Lit *sorrows*
[a]Ps 34:18; 51:17; Is 61:1
[b]Job 5:18; Is 30:26; Ezek 34:16

**Psalm 147:4**
[1]Or *calls them all by* their *names*
[a]Gen 15:5
[b]Is 40:26

**Psalm 147:5**
[1]Lit *innumerable*
[a]Ps 48:1; 145:3
[b]Is 40:28

**Psalm 147:6**
[1]Or *relieves*
[a]Ps 37:24; 146:8, 9

**Psalm 147:7**
[a]Ps 33:2; 95:1, 2

**Psalm 147:8**
[1]Lit *spring forth*
[a]Job 26:8
[b]Job 5:10; 38:26; Ps 104:13
[c]Job 38:27; Ps 104:14

**Psalm 147:9**
[a]Ps 104:27, 28; 145:15
[b]Job 38:41; Matt 6:26

**Psalm 147:10**
[a]Ps 33:17
[b]1 Sam 16:7

**Psalm 147:11**
[a]Ps 149:4
[b]Ps 33:18

**Psalm 147:13**
[a]Neh 3:3; 7:3
[b]Ps 37:26

**Psalm 147:14**
[1]Lit *your borders peace*
[2]Lit *fat*
[a]Ps 29:11; Is 54:13; 60:17, 18
[b]Ps 132:15
[c]Deut 32:14; Ps 81:16

**Psalm 147:15**
[a]Job 37:12; Ps 148:5
[b]Ps 104:4

**Psalm 147:16**
[a]Job 37:6; Ps 148:8
[b]Job 38:29

**Psalm 147:17**
[a]Job 37:10
[b]Job 37:9

**Psalm 147:18**
[a]Ps 33:9; 107:20; 147:15
[b]Ps 107:25

**Psalm 147:19**

[a]Deut 33:3, 4
[b]Mal 4:4


**Psalm 147:20**
[1]Or *Hallelujah!*
[2]Heb *YAH*
[a]Deut 4:7, 8, 32-34; Rom 3:1, 2
[b]Ps 79:6; Jer 10:25

## Targum

**Psa. 147:1** Hallelujah! For it is good to make music in the presence of our God, for it is pleasant, praise is comely. [2] The LORD is the builder of Jerusalem, he will gather the exiles of Jerusalem. [3] Who heals the broken hearted, and applies bandages to their hurts. [4] He numbers the sum of the stars, calling them all by name. [5] Great is our lord and abundant in power; there is no sum of his intelligence. [6] The LORD supports the meek, he humbles the wicked to the ground. [7] Sing praise in the presence of the LORD with thanksgiving; make music in the presence of our God with the harp. [8] Who covers the heavens with clouds, who prepares rain for the earth, who makes grass grow on the mountains. [9] He gives to the beast its food, to the young of the raven that cry out. [10] He will not desire the strength of those who ride on horses; he will take no pleasure in the thighs of swift men. [11] The LORD takes pleasure in those that fear him, who wait long for his goodness. [12] Praise, O Jerusalem, the LORD, praise your God, O Zion. [13] For he has strengthened the bars of your gates, he has blessed your sons in your midst. [14] Who has set peace at your border, he will satisfy you with the fat of wheat. [15] Who sends his word to the earth, with speed his speech will run. [16] Who gives snow as white as wool, he will scatter frost like ash. [17] Who casts his hail parceled out as crumbs; who is able to stand before his cold? [18] He will send the east wind of his wrath and melt them; he will make his wind blow [and] waters flow. [19] Who tells the words of Torah to Jacob, his statutes and judgments to Israel. [20] He has not acted so with every people; he did not tell them his judgments. Hallelujah!

## Spiritual Awareness

### Introduction

This Psalm was written during the rebuilding of Jerusalem after the Babylonian Exile. The Psalmist writes that the LORD is the builder of Jerusalem. The LORD will gather the outcasted Jews one day. At that time the people needed to praise the LORD and rejoice at the restoration of Israel. The city and Temple were far from complete when the Psalm was written.

### Notes on this Psalm

This Psalm praised the LORD for the rebuilding of Jerusalem. What someone can learn spiritually from this time in history is that a person experiences a "dark night of the soul," placing reliance in the LORD will allow the LORD to rebuild the person. No one is ever lost to the LORD. It is whether the person allows the LORD to take control for a while and help get the person back on track.

# Psalm 148

| New American Standard 1995 | Hebrew |
|---|---|
| 1     Praise the LORD!<br>Praise the LORD from the heavens;<br>    Praise Him in the heights!<br>2     Praise Him, all His angels;<br>    Praise Him, all His hosts!<br>3     Praise Him, sun and moon;<br>    Praise Him, all stars of light!<br>4     Praise Him, highest heavens,<br>    And the waters that are above the heavens!<br>5     Let them praise the name of the LORD,<br>    For He commanded and they were created.<br>6     He has also established them forever and ever;<br>    He has made a decree which will not pass away.<br><br>7     Praise the LORD from the Earth,<br>    Sea monsters and all deeps;<br>8     Fire and hail, snow and clouds;<br>    Stormy wind, fulfilling His word;<br>9     Mountains and all hills;<br>    Fruit trees and all cedars;<br>10     Beasts and all cattle;<br>    Creeping things and winged fowl;<br>11     Kings of the Earth and all peoples;<br>    Princes and all judges of the Earth;<br>12     Both young men and virgins;<br>    Old men and children.<br><br>13     Let them praise the name of the LORD, | הַלְלוּ יָהּ ׀ הַלְלוּ אֶת־יְהוָה מִן־<br>הַשָּׁמַיִם הַלְלוּהוּ בַּמְּרוֹמִים: 2<br>הַלְלוּהוּ כָל־מַלְאָכָיו הַלְלוּהוּ כָּל־<br>צְבָאָו [צְבָאָיו:] 3 הַלְלוּהוּ שֶׁמֶשׁ<br>וְיָרֵחַ הַלְלוּהוּ כָּל־כּוֹכְבֵי אוֹר: 4<br>הַלְלוּהוּ שְׁמֵי הַשָּׁמָיִם וְהַמַּיִם אֲשֶׁר<br>מֵעַל הַשָּׁמָיִם: 5 יְהַלְלוּ אֶת־שֵׁם<br>יְהוָה כִּי הוּא צִוָּה וְנִבְרָאוּ: 6<br>וַיַּעֲמִידֵם לָעַד לְעוֹלָם חָק־נָתַן<br>וְלֹא יַעֲבוֹר: 7 הַלְלוּ אֶת־יְהוָה מִן־<br>הָאָרֶץ תַּנִּינִים וְכָל־תְּהֹמוֹת: 8 אֵשׁ<br>וּבָרָד שֶׁלֶג וְקִיטוֹר רוּחַ סְעָרָה<br>עֹשָׂה דְבָרוֹ: 9 הֶהָרִים וְכָל־גְּבָעוֹת<br>עֵץ פְּרִי וְכָל־אֲרָזִים: 10 הַחַיָּה<br>וְכָל־בְּהֵמָה רֶמֶשׂ וְצִפּוֹר כָּנָף: 11<br>מַלְכֵי־אֶרֶץ וְכָל־לְאֻמִּים שָׂרִים<br>וְכָל־שֹׁפְטֵי אָרֶץ: 12 בַּחוּרִים וְגַם־<br>בְּתוּלוֹת זְקֵנִים עִם־נְעָרִים: 13<br>יְהַלְלוּ ׀ אֶת־שֵׁם יְהוָה כִּי־נִשְׂגָּב<br>שְׁמוֹ לְבַדּוֹ הוֹדוֹ עַל־אֶרֶץ וְשָׁמָיִם:<br>14 וַיָּרֶם קֶרֶן ׀ לְעַמּוֹ תְּהִלָּה לְכָל־<br>חֲסִידָיו לִבְנֵי יִשְׂרָאֵל עַם־קְרֹבוֹ<br>הַלְלוּ־יָהּ: |

<table>
<tr><td>

For His name alone is exalted;
His glory is above Earth and Heaven.
14 And He has lifted up a horn for His people,
Praise for all His godly ones;
*Even* for the sons of Israel, a people near to Him.
Praise the LORD!

</td><td></td></tr>
</table>

## Targum

**Psa. 148:1** Hallelujah! Praise the LORD, holy creatures in Heaven; praise him, all hosts of angels on high. ² Praise him, all angels that minister in his presence; praise him, all his hosts. ³ Praise him, sun and moon; praise him, all stars of light. ⁴ Praise him, Heaven of heavens, and the waters that are suspended by his word above the heavens. ⁵ Let them praise the name of the LORD, for he commanded and they were created. ⁶ And he established them for ages upon ages; he gave a decree and none will violate it. ⁷ Praise the LORD in the Earth, sea serpents and all abysses. ⁸ Fire and hail, snow and vapor, storm wind fulfilling his command; ⁹ Mountains and all hills, [every] tree that produces fruit, and all cedars; ¹⁰ Animals and every beast, creeping things and the winged bird that flies; ¹¹ Kings of the Earth and all peoples; rulers and all judges of the Earth. ¹² Lads and even girls, old men and youths; ¹³ Let them praise the name of the LORD, for his name is mighty, he alone; his praise is over Earth and Heaven. ¹⁴ And he has lifted up glory for his people, praise for all his pious ones, for the children of Israel, the people who are close to him: Praise the LORD!

## Summary of the Psalm

This Psalm speaks about when the Gentile nations of the world will receive the knowledge of the LORD. When this happens, the Universe, all living things, from the heights to low places, will come together in praise of the Creator. The Psalm concludes with the rise of Israel, which will guarantee to all people who dedicate themselves to the LORD that they will receive recognition from Heaven for their good deeds.

The LORD's creation is portrayed as two spheres. The Spiritual (celestial) sphere and the terrestrial sphere. Ancient people believed that the celestial sphere was the Heavens. In this sphere, everything was spiritual. On Earth, the LORD's creation is the material world. The terrestrial world will come together one day, Jews, Gentiles, and the creatures of the Earth, to sing a hymn of praise to the LORD as Creator, Preserver, and Lawgiver. The Gentiles will become a part of Israel through their good deeds and dedication to the LORD. All peoples and nations will become one people and one nation.

## Verses One to Six

| New American Standard 1995 | Hebrew |
|---|---|
| 1 Praise the LORD!<br>Praise the LORD from the heavens;<br>Praise Him in the heights!<br>2 Praise Him, all His angels;<br>Praise Him, all His hosts!<br>3 Praise Him, sun and moon;<br>Praise Him, all stars of light!<br>4 Praise Him, highest heavens,<br>And the waters that are above the heavens!<br>5 Let them praise the name of the LORD,<br>For He commanded and they were created.<br>6 He has also established them forever and ever;<br>He has made a decree which will not pass away. | הַלְלוּ יָהּ ׀ הַלְלוּ אֶת־יְהוָה מִן־<br>הַשָּׁמַיִם הַלְלוּהוּ בַּמְּרוֹמִים׃ ²<br>הַלְלוּהוּ כָל־מַלְאָכָיו הַלְלוּהוּ כָּל־<br>צְבָאוֹ הַלְלוּהוּ שֶׁמֶשׁ ³ [צְבָאָיו]׃<br>וְיָרֵחַ הַלְלוּהוּ כָּל־כּוֹכְבֵי אוֹר׃ ⁴<br>הַלְלוּהוּ שְׁמֵי הַשָּׁמָיִם וְהַמַּיִם אֲשֶׁר<br>מֵעַל הַשָּׁמָיִם ⁵ ׀ יְהַלְלוּ אֶת־שֵׁם׃<br>יְהוָה כִּי הוּא צִוָּה וְנִבְרָאוּ׃ ⁶<br>וַיַּעֲמִידֵם לָעַד לְעוֹלָם חָק־נָתַן<br>וְלֹא יַעֲבוֹר׃ |

## Verse Analysis

מִן־הַשָּׁמַיִם (min hashamayim) means "from the Heavens." The usage of שָׁמַיִם falls into two broad categories, 1) the physical heavens and 2) the heavens as the abode of God. In verse one, the Heavens are referring to the physical heavens and the creatures of the Heavens. The luminaries, sun, moon, and stars will join together with the angels and the Heavenly Host to give one considerable praise to the LORD. The celestial world is something that is a mystery to humans. Yes, today, we do understand that the celestial bodies are a part of Malkhut (the physical realm). For ancient people, they did not understand this. For them, everything above the blue sky represented Heaven. The celestial world today is not a part of the spiritual world. The Sefirot Keter to Yesod are the Upper and Lower waters of the spiritual realm. All the Sefirot, the Hebrew Letters, the angels, and every spiritual entity praise the LORD. Our Ruach came from the Lower Waters of the Tree of Life, and one day each of us will return there to be a part of the spiritual world, which is in constant praise of the LORD.

כָּל־כּוֹכְבֵי אוֹר׃ (kal coc'ver ohr) – means "stars of light." This phrase is referring to the fixed stars in the sky that project their light upon the Earth. The fixed stars are referred to as the luminaries.

וְהַמַּיִם אֲשֶׁר ׀ מֵעַל הַשָּׁמָיִם׃ (v'hamayim asher mel hashamayim) – means "the waters above the heavens." This phrase indicates that the psalmist believed that there are worlds still being created today. These unknown bodies are still underwater, as was the Earth at the beginning of creation. The Sages have believed that the LORD's creation process has never stopped. It will continue throughout time. Galaxies are being formed and created even now. Stars explode, and new stars are born. The process of creation is a never-ending process.

In verse one, the psalmist reminds us that the celestial bodies are closely related to the LORD because they are a part of the Heavens. The creatures of Earth are far removed from the presence of the LORD because these things exist in the material world. However, the LORD's power and presence can be felt and seen in Malkhut. The heavenly message from the LORD to humans can be heard by those who are devoted to serving the LORD and praise His holy name.

The bright stars of verse three are described in the Talmud (Bava Basra 8b) as elementary school teachers. Our youth depend on teachers for their education. Youth will learn about the LORD by having teachers. Parents are the best teachers for this purpose. The parents must teach their children about the LORD. If the LORD's teachings are not passed from one generation to another, in time, humankind will not know of the LORD. The LORD will always be present in Malkhut through His Light. Without people performing the Mitzvot of the Torah, then the blessings from Heaven will cease to come down from Yesod. The cycle of blessings is that the LORD sends them to Malkhut. People, in turn, share the blessing by performing the Mitzvot of the Torah. This act sends praises back to the LORD through Yesod. For each praise, the LORD returns blessings. As long as there are people devout to the LORD, the cycle of blessings will always continue.

In verse five, the psalmist reminds us of how important it is to remember that the LORD created the Tree of Life by uttering a few words. The LORD developed the complexity of the Tree of Life. A few words found in the first verses of Genesis, the ten Sefirot, the Hebrew letters, and all spiritual entities were created.

## Verse Rewrite Emphasizing Spiritual Awareness

The English translation from the New American Standard is adequate for the spiritual awareness of this Psalm

## Verses Seven to Fourteen

| New American Standard 1995 | Hebrew |
|---|---|
| 7 Praise the LORD from the Earth, Sea monsters and all deeps; 8 Fire and hail, snow and clouds; Stormy wind, fulfilling His word; 9 Mountains and all hills; Fruit trees and all cedars; 10 Beasts and all cattle; Creeping things and winged fowl; 11 Kings of the Earth and all peoples; Princes and all judges of the Earth; 12 Both young men and virgins; Old men and children. 13 Let them praise the name of the LORD, For His name alone is exalted; His glory is above Earth and Heaven. 14 And He has lifted up a horn for His people, Praise for all His godly ones; *Even* for the sons of Israel, a people near to Him. Praise the LORD! | הַלְלוּ אֶת־יְהוָה מִן־הָאָרֶץ תַּנִּינִים ⁷ וְכָל־תְּהֹמוֹת ׃ אֵשׁ וּבָרָד שֶׁלֶג ⁸ וְקִיטוֹר רוּחַ סְעָרָה עֹשָׂה דְבָרוֹ ׃ ⁹ הֶהָרִים וְכָל־גְּבָעוֹת עֵץ פְּרִי וְכָל־ אֲרָזִים ׃ ¹⁰ הַחַיָּה וְכָל־בְּהֵמָה רֶמֶשׂ וְצִפּוֹר כָּנָף ׃ ¹¹ מַלְכֵי־אֶרֶץ וְכָל־ לְאֻמִּים שָׂרִים וְכָל־שֹׁפְטֵי אָרֶץ ׃ ¹² בַּחוּרִים וְגַם־בְּתוּלוֹת זְקֵנִים עִם־ נְעָרִים ׃ ¹³ יְהַלְלוּ אֶת־שֵׁם יְהוָה כִּי־נִשְׂגָּב שְׁמוֹ לְבַדּוֹ הוֹדוֹ עַל־ אֶרֶץ וְשָׁמָיִם ׃ ¹⁴ וַיָּרֶם קֶרֶן לְעַמּוֹ תְּהִלָּה לְכָל־חֲסִידָיו לִבְנֵי יִשְׂרָאֵל עַם־קְרֹבוֹ הַלְלוּ־יָהּ ׃ |

## Verses Analysis

קִיטוֹר (keetor) – means "smoke." In this Psalm, it is translated as clouds. Hirsch says

that means "mist" or vapor." If the word is understood as a mist, then it could be referring to fog. Thick fog and smoke give the same results. It is difficult and sometimes impossible to see through a fog.

Everything on Earth, in the realm of Malkhut, will praise the LORD. Some events happen in Malkhut that can cause destruction. Thunderstorms can burn down houses. Tornadoes can destroy crops. These events need to be viewed as the negative energy from the left column. Gevurah and Hod generate negative energy that is sent to Malkhut. Negative energy has its value in Malkhut. The world cannot exist without the three energies from the Tree of Life. Sadly negative energy can cause destruction. However, negative energy, for example, electricity, is a good thing. Humankind has to learn how to harness negative energy for its advantage. History tells us that humans have used negative energy to hurt and control each other. If too much negative energy accumulates within a person, the Klippot of evil can form. The brutal dictators of history all had the Klippot surrounding them. These people could not see that what they were doing was evil and against the LORD's decrees. It is next to impossible for positive energy alone to break through a Klippot. Eventually, dictators are overthrown. Unfortunately, it takes many resources to accomplish this.

Verse twelve connects young maidens and young men. Generally speaking, the young want to make themselves attractive to each other. Concentrating on the LORD's ways is easily made a minor consideration so that the young maiden and man can fall in love. During the days of the Messiah, even the young will turn away from their Nefesh's (the flesh) to dedicate themselves to praising and honoring the LORD. The young and the old will learn from each other how best to serve and praise the LORD.

Verse thirteen says that when the Messiah arrives and leads the world, the Kings and other persons in authority will give up their power. They will serve the Messiah, who will show all the world's peoples how to serve the LORD with praise and song.

## Complete Psalm Rewrite Emphasizing Spiritual Awareness

The New American Standard has a reasonable translation of this section except for verse fourteen. Hirsch's translation offers a better view of the spiritual awareness of the verse.

14 And He lifted up the horn – the praiseworthy heights that Yisrael achieved – for His people, which in turn are praised by all those [of the nations] who are devoted to Him and who praise the children of Yisrael as the people who have been close to Him from the beginning: Halleluyah.

# Psalm 149

| New American Standard 1995 | Hebrew |
|---|---|

**Psa. 149:1**  [1]Praise [2]the LORD!
Sing to the LORD a [a]new song,
*And* His praise [b]in the congregation of the godly ones.
[2] Let Israel be glad in [a]his Maker;
Let the sons of Zion rejoice in their [b]King.
[3] Let them praise His name with [a]dancing;
Let them sing praises to Him with [b]timbrel and lyre.
[4] For the LORD [a]takes pleasure in His people;
He will [b]beautify the afflicted ones with salvation.

**Psa. 149:5**  Let the [a]godly ones exult in glory;
Let them [b]sing for joy on their beds.
[6] *Let* the [a]high praises of God *be* in their [1]mouth,
And a [b]two-edged [c]sword in their hand,
[7] To [a]execute vengeance on the nations
And punishment on the peoples,
[8] To bind their kings [a]with chains
And their [b]nobles with fetters of iron,
[9] To [a]execute on them the judgment written;
This is an [b]honor for all His godly ones.
[1]Praise [2]the LORD!

**Psa. 149:1** הַלְלוּ יָהּ ׀ שִׁירוּ לַיהוָה שִׁיר
חָדָשׁ תְּהִלָּתוֹ בִּקְהַל חֲסִידִים׃ [2] יִשְׂמַח
יִשְׂרָאֵל בְּעֹשָׂיו בְּנֵי־צִיּוֹן יָגִילוּ בְמַלְכָּם׃ [3]
יְהַלְלוּ שְׁמוֹ בְמָחוֹל בְּתֹף וְכִנּוֹר יְזַמְּרוּ־לוֹ׃ [4]
כִּי־רוֹצֶה יְהוָה בְּעַמּוֹ יְפָאֵר עֲנָוִים בִּישׁוּעָה׃
[5] יַעְלְזוּ חֲסִידִים בְּכָבוֹד יְרַנְּנוּ עַל־
מִשְׁכְּבוֹתָם׃ [6] רוֹמְמוֹת אֵל בִּגְרוֹנָם וְחֶרֶב
פִּיפִיּוֹת בְּיָדָם׃ [7] לַעֲשׂוֹת נְקָמָה בַּגּוֹיִם
תּוֹכֵחֹת בַּל־אֻמִּים׃ [8] לֶאְסֹר מַלְכֵיהֶם בְּזִקִּים
וְנִכְבְּדֵיהֶם בְּכַבְלֵי בַרְזֶל׃ [9] לַעֲשׂוֹת בָּהֶם ׀
מִשְׁפָּט כָּתוּב הָדָר הוּא לְכָל־חֲסִידָיו הַלְלוּ־
יָהּ׃

|  |  |
|---|---|
|  | 176 |

# References

**Psalm 149:1**
[1]Or *Hallelujah!*
[2]Heb *YAH*
[a]Ps 33:3
[b]Ps 35:18; 89:5

**Psalm 149:2**
[a]Ps 95:6
[b]Judg 8:23; Ps 47:6; Zech 9:9

**Psalm 149:3**
[a]2 Sam 6:14; Ps 150:4
[b]Ex 15:20; Ps 81:2

**Psalm 149:4**
[a]Job 36:11; Ps 16:11; 35:27; 147:11
[b]Ps 132:16; Is 61:3

**Psalm 149:5**
[a]Ps 132:16
[b]Job 35:10; Ps 42:8

**Psalm 149:6**
[1]Lit *throat*
[a]Ps 66:17
[b]Heb 4:12
[c]Neh 4:17

**Psalm 149:7**
[a]Ezek 25:17; Mic 5:15

**Psalm 149:8**
[a]Job 36:8
[b]Nah 3:10

**Psalm 149:9**
[1]Or *Hallelujah!*
[2]Heb *YAH*

*a*Deut 7:12; Ezek 28:26
*b*Ps 112:9; 148:14

## Targum

**Psa. 149:1** Sing in the presence of the LORD a new psalm; his praise is in the assembly of the pious. ² They of the house of Israel will rejoice in their maker; the children of Zion will exult in their kings. ³ They will praise his name with dances, with drums and harps they will make music to him. ⁴ For the pleasure of the LORD is in his people; he will glorify the humble with redemption. ⁵ The pious will revel in glory; they will meditate upon their beds. ⁶ The psalms of God are in their throats, and in their hands like a two-edged sword. ⁷ To wreak vengeance on the Gentiles, rebuke among the nations. ⁸ To bind their kings with chains, and their nobles with fetters of iron. ⁹ To execute on them the judgment written in the Torah; this is glory for all his pious ones. Hallelujah!

## Spiritual Awareness

Introduction

This Psalmist informs us that the praise Psalms are only the beginning of what must be a continuous development of praises for the LORD. It is the perpetual destiny of Israel to praise the LORD. Every new generation meets new challenges and dilemmas. The LORD provides Divine assistance for the solving of any problem.

Notes on this Psalm

Praise the LORD in everything. It is that simple.

# Psalm 150

| New American Standard 1995 | Hebrew |
| --- | --- |
| **Psa. 150:1**  [1]Praise [2]the LORD!<br>Praise God in His [a]sanctuary;<br>Praise Him in His mighty [3][b]expanse.<br>[2] Praise Him for His [a]mighty deeds;<br>Praise Him according to His excellent [b]greatness.<br><br>**Psa. 150:3** Praise Him with [a]trumpet sound;<br>Praise Him with [b]harp and lyre.<br>[4] Praise Him with [a]timbrel and dancing;<br>Praise Him with [b]stringed instruments and [c]pipe.<br>[5] Praise Him with loud [a]cymbals;<br>Praise Him with resounding cymbals.<br>[6] Let [a]everything that has breath praise [1]the LORD.<br>[2]Praise [1]the LORD! | **Psa. 150:1** הַלְלוּ יָהּ ׀ הַלְלוּ־אֵל בְּקָדְשׁוֹ<br>הַלְלוּהוּ בִּרְקִיעַ עֻזּוֹ : 2 הַלְלוּהוּ בִגְבוּרֹתָיו<br>הַלְלוּהוּ כְּרֹב גֻּדְלוֹ : 3 הַלְלוּהוּ בְּתֵקַע שׁוֹפָר<br>הַלְלוּהוּ בְּנֵבֶל וְכִנּוֹר : 4 הַלְלוּהוּ בְתֹף<br>וּמָחוֹל הַלְלוּהוּ בְּמִנִּים וְעוּגָב : 5 הַלְלוּהוּ<br>בְצִלְצְלֵי־שָׁמַע הַלְלוּהוּ בְּצִלְצְלֵי תְרוּעָה : 6<br>כֹּל הַנְּשָׁמָה תְּהַלֵּל יָהּ הַלְלוּ־יָהּ : |

# References

**Psalm 150:1**
[1]Or *Hallelujah!*
[2]Heb *YAH*
[3]Or *firmament*
[a]Ps 73:17; 102:19
[b]Ps 19:1

**Psalm 150:2**
[a]Ps 145:12
[b]Deut 3:24; Ps 145:3

**Psalm 150:3**
[a]Ps 98:6
[b]Ps 33:2

**Psalm 150:4**
[a]Ps 149:3
[b]Ps 45:8; Is 38:20
[c]Gen 4:21; Job 21:12

**Psalm 150:5**
[a]2 Sam 6:5; 1 Chr 13:8; 15:16; Ezra 3:10; Neh 12:27

**Psalm 150:6**
[1]Heb *YAH*
[2]Or *Hallelujah!*
[a]Ps 103:22; 145:21

## Targum

**Psa. 150:1** Hallelujah! Praise God in his sanctuary, praise him in the firmament of his strength. [2] Praise him for his mighty deeds, praise him according to his abundant greatness. [3] Praise him with the sounding of the trumpet, praise him with harps and lyres. [4] Praise him with drums and with dances, praise him with flutes and pipes. [5] Praise him with cymbals that sound alone; praise him with cymbals that sound with shouting. [6] Every breath will sing praise to God. Hallelujah!

## Spiritual Awareness

Introduction

This Psalm summarizes the Book of Psalms.

Notes on this Psalm

The development of the spiritual is the most important a person does during their lifetime. The Zohar says that the soul is sent to Malkut and joined with flesh to learn about the LORD. $1/5^{th}$ of the soul is the flesh. It is a fight between materialism and spiritualism that life is all about. Remember that one day you will return to the Lower Waters. Will you be ready?

# APPENDIX

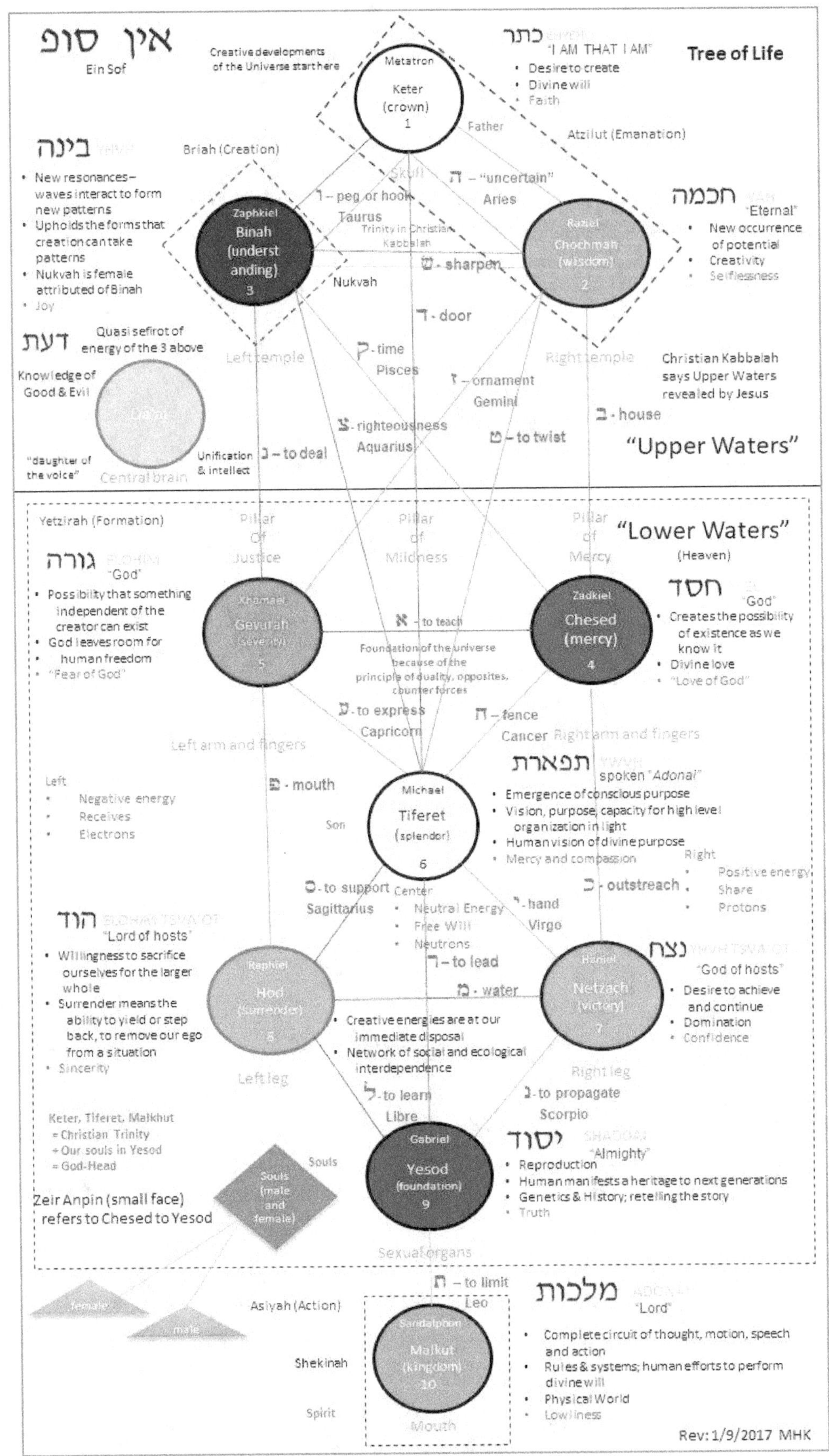

אין סוף
Ein Sof
Creative developments of the Universe start here
כתר
"I AM THAT I AM"
Desire to create
Divine will
Faith
Tree of Life
Metatron
Keter (crown) 1
Father
Atzilut (Emanation)
בינה
New resonances – waves interact to form new patterns
Upholds the forms that creation can take patterns
Nukvah is female attributed of Binah
Joy
Briah (Creation)
ו – peg or hook
Taurus
Trinity in Christian Kabbalah
Zaphkiel
Binah (understanding) 3
Nukvah
ה – "uncertain"
Aries
ש - sharpen
ד - door
Raziel
Chochmah (wisdom) 2
חכמה
"Eternal"
New occurrence of potential
Creativity
Selflessness
דעת
Quasi sefirot of energy of the 3 above
Knowledge of Good & Evil
Daat
"daughter of the voice"
Left temple
Central brain
ק - time
Pisces
ז – ornament
Gemini
צ - righteousness
Aquarius
נ – to deal
Unification & intellect
Right temple
ב - house
ט – to twist
Christian Kabbalah says Upper Waters revealed by Jesus
"Upper Waters"
Yetzirah (Formation)
Pillar Of Justice
Pillar of Mildness
Pillar of Mercy
"Lower Waters"
(Heaven)
גורה
"God"
Possibility that something independent of the creator can exist
God leaves room for human freedom
"Fear of God"
Khamael
Gevurah (severity) 5
א - to teach
Foundation of the universe because of the principle of duality, opposites, counter forces
Zadkiel
Chesed (mercy) 4
חסד
"God"
Creates the possibility of existence as we know it
Divine love
"Love of God"
ס - to express
Capricorn
ח – fence
Cancer
Right arm and fingers
Left arm and fingers
תפארת
spoken "Adonai"
Emergence of conscious purpose
Vision, purpose, capacity for high level organization in light
Human vision of divine purpose
Mercy and compassion
Left
Negative energy
Receives
Electrons
פ - mouth
Michael
Tiferet (splendor) 6
Son
Right
Positive energy
Share
Protons
הוד
"Lord of hosts"
Willingness to sacrifice ourselves for the larger whole
Surrender means the ability to yield or step back, to remove our ego from a situation
Sincerity
ס - to support
Center
Sagittarius
Neutral Energy
Free Will
Neutrons
י - hand
Virgo
כ - outreach
ר - to lead
מ - water
Raphiel
Hod (surrender) 8
Creative energies are at our immediate disposal
Network of social and ecological interdependence
Haniel
Netzach (victory) 7
נצח
"God of hosts"
Desire to achieve and continue
Domination
Confidence
Left leg
ל - to learn
Libre
Right leg
צ - to propagate
Scorpio
Keter, Tiferet, Malkhut = Christian Trinity + Our souls in Yesod = God-Head
Zeir Anpin (small face) refers to Chesed to Yesod
Souls
Souls (male and female)
Souls
Gabriel
Yesod (foundation) 9
יסוד
"Almighty"
Reproduction
Human manifests a heritage to next generations
Genetics & History; retelling the story
Truth
Sexual organs
female
male
Asiyah (Action)
Shekinah
Spirit
ת – to limit
Leo
Sandalphon
Malkut (kingdom) 10
Mouth
מלכות
"Lord"
Complete circuit of thought, motion, speech and action
Rules & systems; human efforts to perform divine will
Physical World
Lowliness
Rev: 1/9/2017 MHK

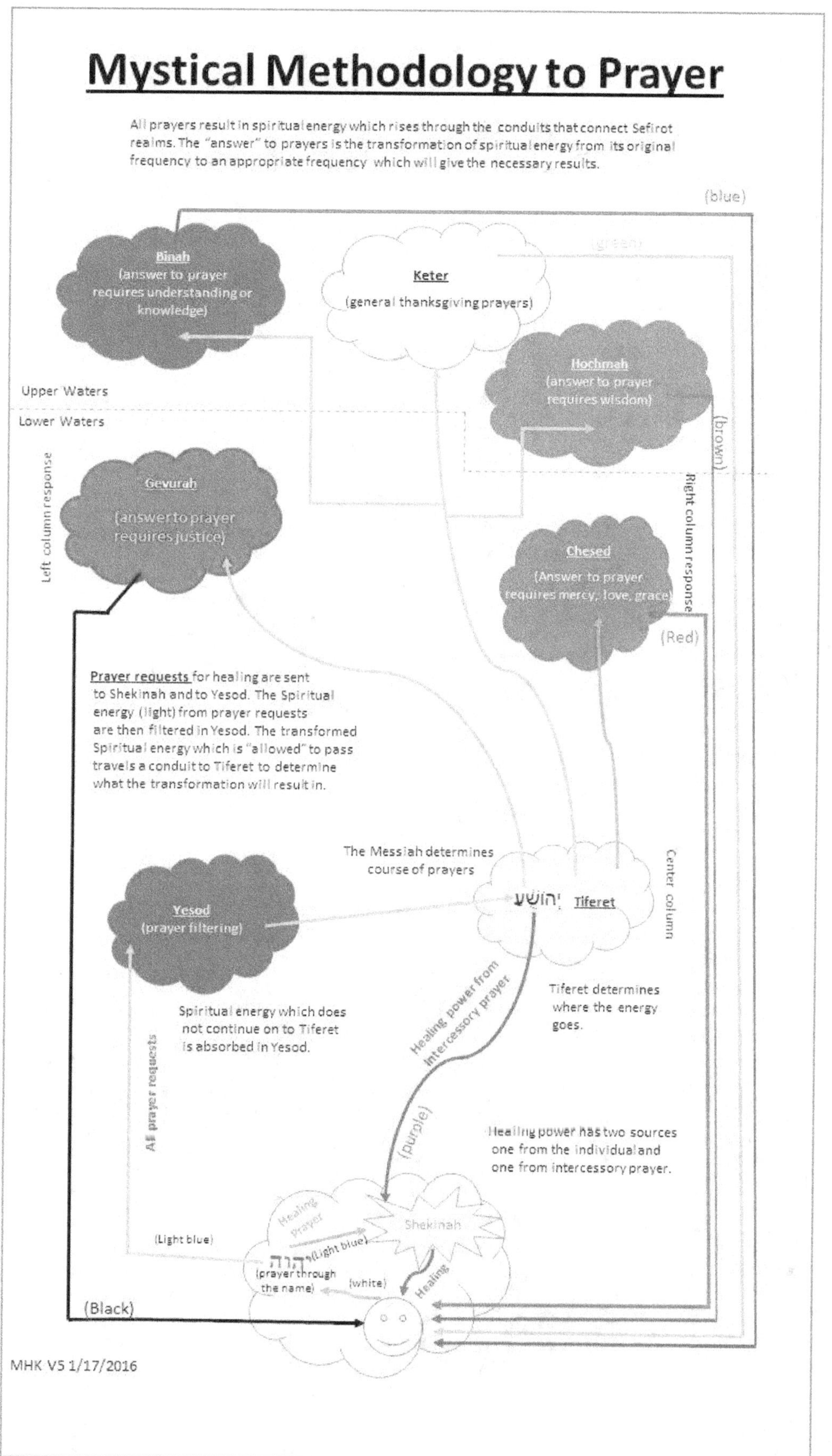
Mystical Methodology to Prayer
All prayers result in spiritual energy which rises through the conduits that connect Sefirot realms. The "answer" to prayers is the transformation of spiritual energy from its original frequency to an appropriate frequency which will give the necessary results.
(blue)
(green)
Binah
(answer to prayer requires understanding or knowledge)
Keter
(general thanksgiving prayers)
Hochmah
(answer to prayer requires wisdom)
Upper Waters
Lower Waters
(brown)
Left column response
Gevurah
(answer to prayer requires justice)
Chesed
(Answer to prayer requires mercy, love, grace)
Right column response
(Red)
Prayer requests for healing are sent to Shekinah and to Yesod. The Spiritual energy (light) from prayer requests are then filtered in Yesod. The transformed Spiritual energy which is "allowed" to pass travels a conduit to Tiferet to determine what the transformation will result in.
The Messiah determines course of prayers
יהושע   Tiferet
Center column
Yesod
(prayer filtering)
Tiferet determines where the energy goes.
Healing power from intercessory prayer
Spiritual energy which does not continue on to Tiferet is absorbed in Yesod.
All prayer requests
(purple)
Healing power has two sources one from the individual and one from intercessory prayer.
Healing Prayer
Shekinah
(Light blue)
(Light blue)
יהוה
(prayer through the name)
(white)
Healing
(Black)
MHK V5 1/17/2016

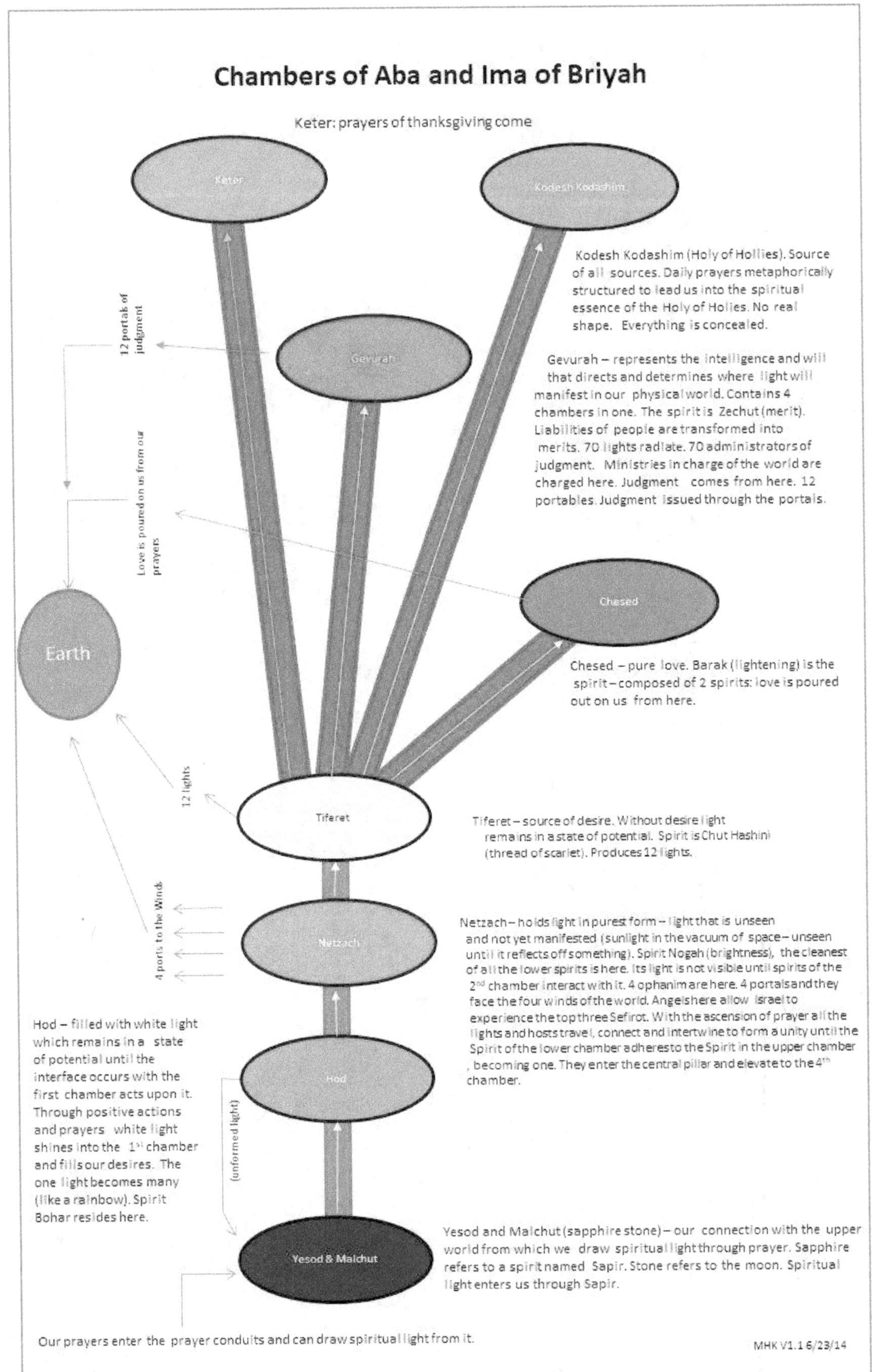


Chambers of Aba and Ima of Briyah

Keter: prayers of thanksgiving come

Keter

Kodesh Kodashim

12 portals of judgment

Gevurah

Love is poured on us from our prayers

Chesed

Earth

Kodesh Kodashim (Holy of Hollies). Source of all sources. Daily prayers metaphorically structured to lead us into the spiritual essence of the Holy of Hollies. No real shape. Everything is concealed.

Gevurah – represents the intelligence and will that directs and determines where light will manifest in our physical world. Contains 4 chambers in one. The spirit is Zechut (merit). Liabilities of people are transformed into merits. 70 lights radiate. 70 administrators of judgment. Ministries in charge of the world are charged here. Judgment comes from here. 12 portables. Judgment issued through the portals.

Chesed – pure love. Barak (lightening) is the spirit – composed of 2 spirits: love is poured out on us from here.

12 lights

Tiferet

Tiferet – source of desire. Without desire light remains in a state of potential. Spirit is Chut Hashini (thread of scarlet). Produces 12 lights.

4 ports to the Winds

Netzach

Netzach – holds light in purest form – light that is unseen and not yet manifested (sunlight in the vacuum of space – unseen until it reflects off something). Spirit Nogah (brightness), the cleanest of all the lower spirits is here. Its light is not visible until spirits of the 2nd chamber interact with it. 4 ophanim are here. 4 portals and they face the four winds of the world. Angels here allow Israel to experience the top three Sefirot. With the ascension of prayer all the lights and hosts travel, connect and intertwine to form a unity until the Spirit of the lower chamber adheres to the Spirit in the upper chamber, becoming one. They enter the central pillar and elevate to the 4th chamber.

Hod – filled with white light which remains in a state of potential until the interface occurs with the first chamber acts upon it. Through positive actions and prayers white light shines into the 1st chamber and fills our desires. The one light becomes many (like a rainbow). Spirit Bohar resides here.

Hod

(unformed light)

Yesod & Malchut

Yesod and Malchut (sapphire stone) – our connection with the upper world from which we draw spiritual light through prayer. Sapphire refers to a spirit named Sapir. Stone refers to the moon. Spiritual light enters us through Sapir.

Our prayers enter the prayer conduits and can draw spiritual light from it.

MHK V1.1 6/23/14

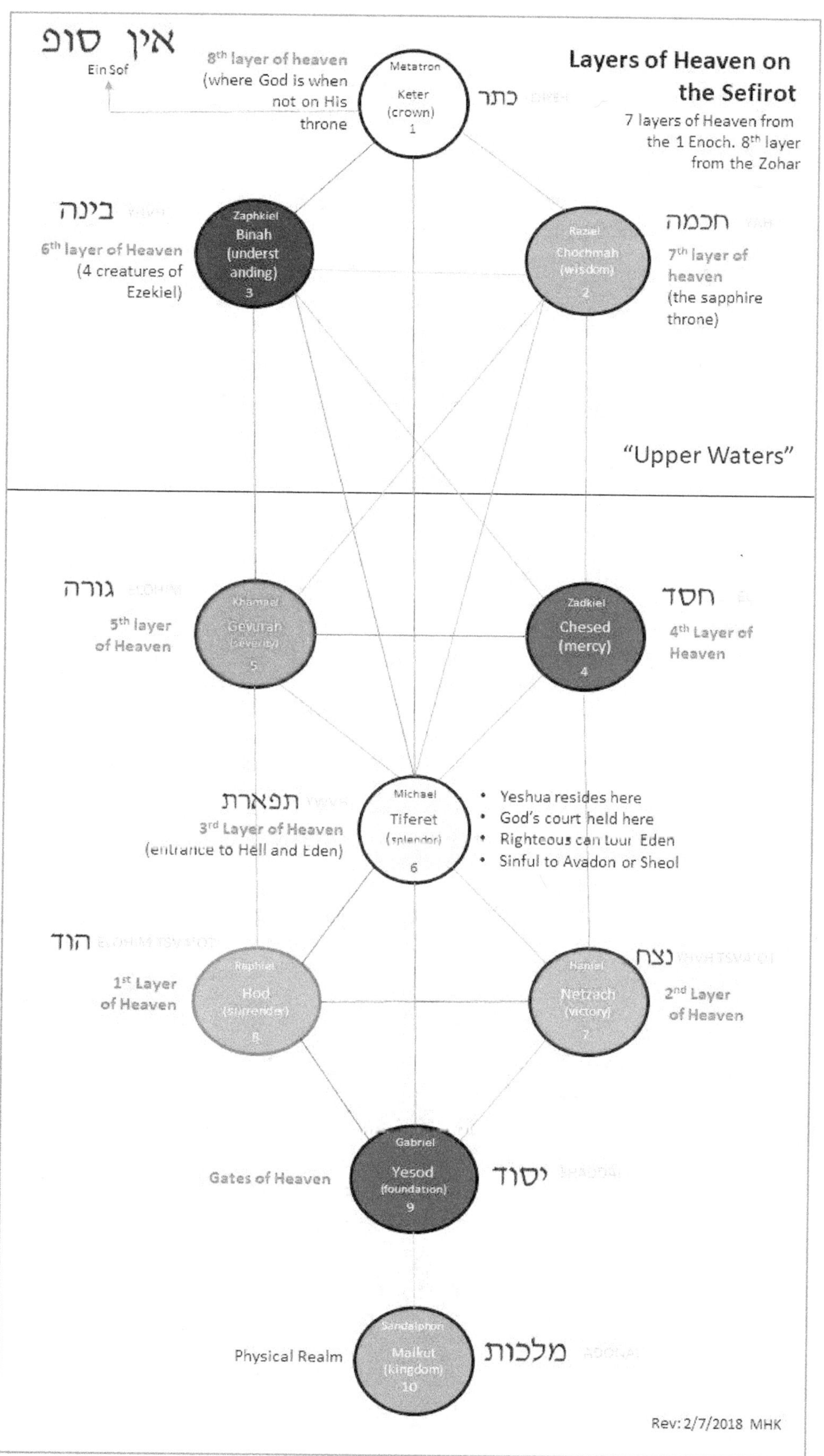

אין סוף
Ein Sof

8th layer of heaven (where God is when not on His throne)

Layers of Heaven on the Sefirot
7 layers of Heaven from the 1 Enoch. 8th layer from the Zohar

Metatron
Keter (crown)
1
כתר

בינה
6th layer of Heaven (4 creatures of Ezekiel)

Zaphkiel
Binah (understanding)
3

Raziel
Chochmah (wisdom)
2

חכמה
7th layer of heaven (the sapphire throne)

"Upper Waters"

גבורה
5th layer of Heaven

Khamael
Gevurah (severity)
5

Zadkiel
Chesed (mercy)
4

חסד
4th Layer of Heaven

תפארת
3rd Layer of Heaven (entrance to Hell and Eden)

Michael
Tiferet (splendor)
6

• Yeshua resides here
• God's court held here
• Righteous can tour Eden
• Sinful to Avadon or Sheol

הוד
1st Layer of Heaven

Raphael
Hod (surrender)
8

Haniel
Netzach (victory)
7

נצח
2nd Layer of Heaven

Gabriel
Yesod (foundation)
9

Gates of Heaven

יסוד

Sandalphon
Malkut (kingdom)
10

Physical Realm

מלכות

Rev: 2/7/2018 MHK

Michael Harvey Koplitz

www.ingramcontent.com/pod-product-compliance
Lightning Source LLC
Chambersburg PA
CBHW080902160726
48000CB00009B/2820